The Mighty Bernard

A Story of St. Bernard of Clairvaux

by

BROTHER EVAN SCHMID, C.S.C.

DUJARIE PRESS

Notre Dame   Indiana

NIHIL OBSTAT

C. F. Brooks, C.S.C.
Censor Deputatus

CUM PERMISSU

Brother Donatus Schmitz, C.S.C.
Provincial

IMPRIMATUR

✠ Most Rev. Leo A. Pursley, D.D.
Bishop of Fort Wayne

After Bellini by Brother Harold Ruplinger, C.S.C.

1

Under bright stars the great stone bulk of Fontaines Castle loomed like a huge shadow over the Burgundy plain; but from one of the dark towers a faint light glimmered. Though it was past midnight, Lady Alice had lighted a candle in her bed chamber.

"Tescelin! Tescelin!" Frightened, Alice tugged at her husband's arm.

"What is it?" the lord mumbled drowsily. "Why aren't you asleep?" As he turned, Tescelin's brown beard glinted in the light—a thick, curly beard, reason for people calling him Tescelin the Tawny.

"I've had a terrible nightmare." Alice spoke in a whisper so as not to arouse the watchman on guard outside the door. "I dreamed that the child I'm bearing was a dog, and that it barked so loudly that I woke up!"

"A dog! And barking!" Lord Tescelin looked sleepily at his wife. "Don't worry over a mere foolish dream. Tell the priest about it tomorrow and he'll explain what it means."

Alice snuffed the candle and crawled into bed, but troubled thoughts kept her tossing and turning until dawn. After Mass early that day, she hurried to the castle priest with her story.

"Remember how David in the psalms said that the very dogs would bark against the enemies of God," her confessor explained. "Your dream means that the child soon to be born will one day be like a watchdog in the Lord's house, the Chuch. The dog's barking, I would say, is an omen that the child will be a great preacher whose golden tongue will heal many souls."

[8]

Comforted by these prophetic words, Lady Alice returned to her household tasks, a daily round of ordering the serfs who cleaned and cooked, and washed clothes, and of spinning fine wool or sewing glistening ornaments of rank on her husband's robes.

Fontaines Castle stood near the town of Dijon in southeast France, the castle and lands held by Tescelin Sorus in fief to the Duke of Burgundy. As vassal of his liege lord the Duke, Tescelin ruled his own domain and served among the Duke's closest advisors. Both the Lord and Lady of Fontaines belonged to the Burgundian nobility by birth, both had their hearts set on fulfilling their duties as Catholics and leaders in society and living in as Christlike a manner as possible. To do this just at the time when France and Europe were emerging from the confused period of history known as the Dark Ages was no easy task, but Tescelin the Tawny and his young wife Alice, who was the daughter of Bernard, Lord of Montbar, had hearts at peace with God and with all men. Now, just about ten years before the twelfth century began, the noble parents, with their two sons Guy and Gerard, awaited another addition to the family—the child Alice had dreamed of.

Great was the rejoicing at Fontaines when in the year 1090 the Lady Alice gave birth to a third son, whom Tescelin decided to name Bernard. At the castle a horde of knights and ladies summoned for the christening marked the joyful event with games of chivalry for the men, delightful gossipy visits for the women. These same friends had occasion in the next few years to repeat their visits, for Lady Alice presented Tescelin with three more sons—named Andrew, Bartholomew, and Nivard—and, last of all, a daughter, named Humbeline.

"Six boys and a girl! Surely you need have no qualms about keeping Fontaines safe from greedy barons," exclaimed Tescelin's friends. "Before you know it, your sons will grow to be six staunch knights ready to tilt the lance with the best of the Duke's men!"

"Do I deny it?" Tescelin stroked his beard, proud of his fine brood. "Why, I'd not trade my children for all of France!" A shadow of worry suddenly darkened his eyes. "But, my friends, these warlike times keep us all, even the children, on our toes. A man's sword—and his God. That's the only protection we have!"

"Ah, yes. What else can one expect but trouble and danger," Tescelin's friends agreed. "The French dukes rival the king in power, and the lesser lords—the counts, earls, barons, and the rest—seem to have nothing to do but fight for one another's castles or fields. War seems to be our most popular amusement."

"Thank God for the Church!" exclaimed Tescelin as the discussion continued. "After the Roman Empire fell and hundreds of years of barbarism and disorder followed, the Church stood as the only bulwark of peace and civilization. Without its work, we'd probably be savages instead of Christian men with fine towns and castles, men redeemed by Our Lord Jesus who must build the kingdom of God on earth and win heaven by holy living."

The wives of knights and lords being entertained at Fontaines Castle clustered around Lady Alice, a woman they all admired and loved.

"Why is it," they asked her, "that you don't send the youngest children out to be nursed by some good castle servant or village woman? It's a custom we all observe."

"Really, I can't allow strangers to bring up my children," Lady Alice explained. "As each one was born, I consecrated them to God, and I don't intend to let being fashionable, slim, or beautiful keep me from a real mother's duty."

Alice's friends said nothing, because they already knew how devoted to her husband and family she was and how she rivaled the very saints in her goodness.

"Lady Alice's children drink her milk and at the same time drink in her virtue too!" they exclaimed to one another.

Tescelin left almost entirely in his wife's hand the rearing of his six sons and one daughter, since affairs of the Duke of Burgundy either on the battlefield or in council, plus the ruling of his own lands, kept the lord of Fontaines often away from home.

"Of course, you'll make monks and nun

of all the children," he joked. "Well I know, sweet lady, that as a girl you wished to be a nun yourself!"

Alice smiled happily. "I have no regrets, my lord, for heeding my parents wish that I marry. As for the children, can one do better than teach them more for heaven than for earth?"

Guy and Gerard, the eldest of the boys, as well as Bernard, Andrew, Bartholomew, Nivard, and tiny Humbeline, idolized their handsome father, and loved the gentle Alice no less. The boys dreamed of feats of arms as they grew up, imitated the knights at their games, and never forgot the adventurous years that lay ahead. Their mother took care to channel these boyish dreams into worthwhile ambitions. "Remember, my sons," she often cautioned, "that for a man who loves God, the world's power, riches, and honors are empty as the very air!"

From their mother the children of Fontaines learned their catechism, their prayers, their habits of virtue. Bernard in particular noticed how often the Lady Alice knelt in the cold chapel for long hours of prayer; how frequently she rode off to visit sick villagers or give alms to poor serfs or wandering beggars.

Alice all the while kept an especially fond eye on her son Bernard, the one she wished above all to see one day a priest at God's altar. And what Alice saw made her particularly grateful: for the boy Bernard could not have been more attractive. His slender figure, golden hair, and charming manners charmed everyone in the castle.

"I sometimes wonder whether Bernard's not the handsomest of all the children," Alice remarked one day to her husband. "Indeed, my lord, I think the boy looks more like you than the other children."

Such transparent flattery made Tescelin chuckle into his beard. "Well, my lady," he said as he kissed her, "he resembles me only in body, then, because I'm certain that Bernard's soul is the image of his mother's."

"He likes to be alone, although he's not a killjoy when it comes to games and fun," the mother went on. "Whenever he gets a *sou,* he gives it away at once. I don't think he ever once disobeyed or flared up in a rage, as boys often do."

More serious for a moment, Tescelin sat down to talk over his plans for Bernard. "Obviously, the child has a quick mind and a talent for study. He's only nine years old now, but I think it's time he enters school somewhere."

"There's the church school at Chatillon a few miles away," Alice said slowly, reluctant to think of losing the lad. "The canons who teach there have already told me they're eager to take him."

Shortly after, young Bernard enrolled in the Chatillon school, where he astonished the master's with his swift progress.

"He's learned to read and write Latin, has tried his hand with good results at poetry, and excels lads far beyond his age," the canons reported after a while to the parents. "He gobbles up theology and philosophy like a hungry eagle. And we've never seen anyone with such a love for the Holy Scriptures—at least not anyone so young!"

Bernard, on the other hand, had something else to report as the years of school passed one by one, interrupted for him only by a few visits home.

"The canons talk about religious matter in a mocking way sometimes," he told his mother, "or try to reason out mysteries of faith that we can't possibly understand."

"They mean no harm. It's the fashionable thing among scholars these days," Alice replied.

"The Catholic faith is above the human mind and the arguments of logic." Bernard's sincere remarks gave his mother a clear indication of how thoughtful he had become. "Who can prove the Holy Trinity exists," Bernard cried, "by using his mind alone? Just let a man try! Really, mother, our Faith is too sacred to play with, even by the scholars!"

"The teachers have told me how you love the Scriptures," Alice said, taking Bernard's arm. "Now keep up the practice of reading them every day, of thinking deeply over what the holy writers say. Nothing better feeds our minds then meditation on Sacred Scripture."

[16]

It was advice Bernard had already made a habit. The Old and New Testaments became almost a second language for him, and what he wrote and taught in later life was like a clover field in which quotations from Holy Writ were the blossoms.

About the time Bernard had entered school, both Guy and Gerard began training for knighthood and military careers. "There's no choice for Burgundian boys, really," Tescelin reminded Lady Alice, "except service with the Duke or service to the Church. When they grew old enough, Andrew and Bartholomew, too, will join the Duke, a prospect that even little Nivard expects to follow."

Though she prayed constantly for her family's welfare, Alice knew that it was almost inevitable that her boys would be men-at-arms. "Everyone in Europe talks of nothing but deeds of valor and knightly exploits of princes and nobles," she remarked to Tescelin.

"They remember the First Crusade, of course," her husband rejoined. "After all, isn't it a glorious thing that French nobles should have captured four provinces in Palestine and held rule over them to this day?"

"The troubadours and minstrels sing of little else." Like everyone in those days, Alice enjoyed hearing the news set to ballad measure and sung to the accompaniment of lutes.

"The Christians in the Holy Land face much danger yet," Tescelin told her. "The forces of Islam—those confounded Mohammedan infidels —are growing more powerful every day, and with all the disorders here at home, who can avoid taking up the sword?"

Busy with his studies, Bernard had little time to dream of knightly prowess, but as he grew into his late teens, an unhappy event at Fontaines brought him a stern reminder that life has difficulties even a boy must face.

Each year on the Feast of St. Ambrose, one of Lady Alice's favorites, she invited all the priests in Dijon and nearby towns to a banquet at the castle. In the year 1110, according to her custom, the invitations were sent as usual, but a few days before the feast, Alice took sick. Medicines gave no help, and on the eve of St. Ambrose's feast day, Lady Alice received the last rites of the Church. Tescelin and the children stood around her bed during her last moments, reciting the prayers for the dying with the priest, prayers in which she, too, joined until, as Alice made the Sign of the Cross, she died.

For all the family at Fontaines, her death was a terrible loss. Most keenly of all because he had been so close to his mother, Bernard now felt his bright, promising world collapsing around him, with even his firm faith in God providing little consolation.

"You're just at the age to fully realize what a mother's love means," Tescelin told the grieving boy. "You must remember that pain and suffering come to all men; thus does the Lord test our love."

Bernard, only nineteen years old when his mother died, now finished his schooling at Chatillon and returned to Fontaines, much in doubt about his future plans.

"Wait to decide," his father counseled. "God will eventually show what He wants you to do."

With Tescelin so often absent from the castle,

Bernard became very much his own master. With his good looks, clever talk, and quick mind, he was the kind of lad the world readily takes to its heart. Simply being the son of a nobleman would have been enough, but Bernard had so many other qualities that made him attractive.

"You're at the very age when the trials of a young man growing into manhood are strongest," Tescelin told him on one occasion. "Life's three great temptations lie around you, ready to strike. The world, the flesh, and the devil—these are the enemies to fight and vanquish."

"True, father," agreed Bernard, "I have learned what these three are. A man's tempted to greed, to sensuality, and to pride—and almost all life's disorders can be listed under one or the other."

One day Bernard spied a woman so lovely that he could hardly tear his eyes away, and as he rode along toward Fontaines, disturbing thoughts regarding her began to race through his mind. On reaching home, he rushed over the fields to a pond of ice-cold water, stripped off his clothes, and stood up to the neck in the freezing water until the temptations disappeared. Some of Tescelin's men, who had been watching the lad, dashed over to the half-dead boy and pulled him out.

Informed of this behavior, Bernard's confessor advised the lad to use more prudence. "But, thank God, nonetheless, that temptations are easier now for you to overcome."

Some weeks afterward, Bernard was riding to visit his brothers, engaged with the Duke's troops in besieging Grancy Castle. As the horse jogged along, Bernard suddenly seemed to glimpse the whole glittering, enticing world passing before his eyes, with all its pitfalls and allures. At the same time, he felt the urge to flee from the dangers the world holds for a man who loves God and desires to be virtuous. "Am I to be a monk?" he asked himself, "or should I be a lawyer or scholar? Does God want me to be a knight like my father, or does He want me to serve the Church?"

Musing on such questions as these, Bernard recalled what he knew of the monks at the Abbey of Cîteaux, a house only twelve miles from Dijon founded in 1098 by Robert of Molesmes. "These monks have restored the Rule of St. Benedict in its primitive form," Bernard thought as he rode along. "Stephen Harding governs the Abbey now, and everyone talks of how holy he and his few monks are."

Seized with a sudden longing, Bernard dismounted before a wayside church and hurried in to pour out his unrest before Christ on the altar. "Direct me, O God," he begged, "that I may discover and follow Thy holy will."

Gradually, a sense of peace stole into his heart—the action of grace flooding his soul. Then and there young Bernard consecrated himself soul and body to the service of God. "I am ready to shoulder whatever cross my Lord and Master chooses to lay upon me," he said half-aloud. "Just as the Crusaders fight for the Lord Christ, so shall I, but in a different garb and manner. I will become a monk at Citeaux."

2

At Grancy Castle Bernard's brothers, weary of the long siege, heard with dismay that the talented Bernard wanted to join the poor monks at Citeaux.

"Don't you realize that these Cistercians have only one aim, to do penance?" they asked.

"Yes, I've learned a great deal about their life in the past few weeks," Bernard answered. "The Cistercian monks follow the Rule of St. Benedict, but more strictly than anyone else.

Their monasteries are built in the wilderness, and the Order owns no property except what the monk's manual labor can provide. Prayer and work—these sum up the monk's life. Their houses are simple and bare, and even the chapels and ceremonies are devoid of ornament or rich display."

"And you want to hide away in such a place," Bernard's brothers argued. "Go back to Fontaines and think seriously about your future, which is too promising to be thrown away."

Nothing could shake Bernard's resolution, nor did Tescelin wish to obstruct the plans God had for his brilliant son, yet the first really to succumb to young Bernard's influence was his uncle Gauldry, a wealthy lord more famed for valor than for virtue.

"I'm ready to follow wherever you lead," Gauldry told his nephew, "and I'll join you as soon as I've distributed my wealth to the poor."

Of the immediate family, Bartholomew was first to heed Bernard's persuasive urging to give up the world for God. Attempts to lead Andrew, however, seemed to have little effect.

"I've just been knighted," Bernard's second younger brother said, "and here you're trying to get me to throw the honor away. I'll have none of it!"

For days, Andrew tried to dodge out of sight whenever Bernard approached; but the time soon came when he too felt God calling. Breathlessly, he rushed to his brother's side to beg that he also might become a devoted knight of the Lord Jesus Christ.

Guy, eldest son of the family, was by now married and the father of two daughters. A good man and prominent in the Duke's court, he yearned to imitate Bernard's example, but his responsibilities were barriers not easily overcome.

"If my lady wife consents," he told Bernard, "I wish to give up the world as you intend to do, yet whenever I mention the subject to her, she weeps and refuses to consider it. Of course, I can't leave her unless she should enter a convent herself."

Enlighted by grace, Bernard told what would happen. "Your wife will either agree to your plan, Guy, or she will die."

"How can you want to leave me? Can both of us not find holiness together?" Guy's wife, who loved her husband, pleaded that he give up his notions. "Without you I cannot go on living!"

So greatly did the young woman grieve that she fell sick, whereupon she sent for Bernard. "As you see, my brother, I'm troubled both in mind and body over what my husband proposes. Yet during these days of sickness the good Lord has enlightened me. Tell my husband that I wish, too, to consecrate my life to the One who calls him."

Together with his brother and sister-in-law, Bernard arranged for settling the household affairs, sending the children to relatives, and putting all in order before Guy and his wife parted. The work completed, Guy became a member of Bernard's little company, and his wife retired to a convent of nuns near Dijon.

Tescelin watched all these occurrences in his family with puzzlement, yet his good heart refused to quail. "If God wishes me to give up my sons, then I must sacrifice my ambitions for them. There's left to me still my second oldest son Gerard, and have I not by my side always young Nivard and sweet little Humbeline?"

"Indeed you have me, father," Gerard angrily exclaimed one day. "I'll have nothing to do with Bernard's mad proposals. Bid me adieu now, good father, for I'm off to join the Burgundian troops."

Gerard's resistance troubled Bernard because he knew it was due to worldliness, so he rode to find his brother where the troops were besieging another castle in the vicinity.

"Though you're a brave soldier whom everybody admires," Bernard told his brother firmly, "you're paying no attention to the vocation to which God calls you."

Gerard turned aside, refusing to listen, but Bernard stepped after him and grabbed his shoulder. "Nothing but misfortune, my brother," he cried, "will open your eyes to the truth!"

"Misfortune! What can happen to me. I fear neither man nor beast!" Irritated, Gerard tried to brush Bernard off.

"The day is coming when this spot I touch will be struck by a lance," said Bernard, "and into the wound will flow the grace that you now reject."

Even as Bernard spoke, a sharp pain pierced Gerard's shoulder, as if someone had plunged a sword there, yet he allowed his face to show no sign. Bernard left the camp, while Gerard resumed his post with the besiegers. During a skirmish a few days later, a lance thrown from the castle ramparts struck him in the very place Bernard had touched. Bleeding and unconscious, Gerard lay on the battlefield until an enemy search party found him and bore him away a prisoner. From the jail, Gerard, slowly recovering from his wounds, managed to send Bernard a message begging him to come at once.

"That I will not do," the younger brother told the messenger. "Go, tell Gerard that his injuries are not fatal, that they will lead him to life, not death!"

For many days the prisoner puzzled over these words, his thoughts turning attentively on all that Bernard had been doing over the past few months at Fontaines. Finally, managing to escape his captors, and certain that he, too, must join his brother on the road to God, Gerard hurried to the castle.

"I've broken the chains that held me," he told Bernard, "now you must help me escape the bonds holding me to the world."

Tescelin's friends gossiped freely over the remarkable events occurring at Fontaines. "Why, Bernard's scarcely twenty years old," they said, "yet he seems to be guide and father to the whole family! Even noblemen of other houses are joining the enterprise."

With his brothers and others of the little band growing up around him, Bernard discussed the best course to follow. "We all desire to live the religious life, but exactly where, and how, we must leave in the hands of God." Drawn as he was to imitate the monks at Citeaux, the young man told what he knew of the Cistercians and their austere life. At the same time he instructed the noble company how to live as truly Christian men, showing some the folly of the world, others the consolation and sweetness to be found in a life dedicated completely to God.

"Every man, and above all Christian men, need to learn the true purpose of human life," he said, "and then to run bravely and steadily toward it. A real man does not exchange a few passing pleasures for the eternal joys that reward faithfulness to Our Lord." When one or another of his followers became doubtful or irresolute, Bernard carefully sought the man out. "Do you wonder that you float between good and evil," he asked, "when you have never set your foot on solid rock? Make a firm resolution right now to give all to Christ, and nothing will be able to turn you away."

Young Hugh of Macon, an intimate friend of Bernard's and a former schoolfellow, felt cut to the heart by the rumors and reports from Fontaines. "I've lost my best friend," he complained, "for Bernard is now lost not only to the world but to me!"

Almost without thinking, the noble Hugh raced off to see for himself what was happening. On meeting, Bernard and he could hardly speak, they were so moved, yet Hugh's resistance crumbled quickly enough. "I swear from this moment on to live for God alone," he cried, "and thus you and I, Bernard, will always be united in the Lord Christ."

Glad to hear this, Bernard did what he could to fix Hugh in his good resolutions. After the young nobleman returned home, however, his devout promises began to waver as the pressure of business and pleasure caught him up again. Bernard heard of it and hurried to a nearby castle where Hugh was a guest, there to find his friend with a group of courtiers huddled under a tree and waiting for a summer shower to pass.

"Come, Hugh," Bernard said as he walked up, "you must wait out the storm with me." Taking his friends arm, Bernard led him along a path toward the open fields. As the storm blew over, he spoke so sweetly and forcefully of the call to serve God that the disquiet in Hugh's soul vanished like the rain clouds burning away under the summer sun. Hugh never again swerved from the path of duty, and this good friend of Bernard's later became the Abbot of Pontigny, the second daughter house of Citeaux, and then the Bishop of Auxerre.

Including his brothers, the thirty young noblemen now gathered under Bernard's leadership assembled for discussions and prayers at a house at Chatillon, the town where Bernard had attended school. A member of the company explained one day to his parents what manner of life the little band was following.

"We wear ordinary clothes, and like real monks practice the vows of poverty, chastity, and obedience. There's strict observance of the Church fasts and long periods of prayer and meditation. Charitable work in the town and countryside keeps us busy when we're not assembled in the church."

"No matter what good we might do," Bernard warned the company, "we must beware never to take pride in our way of life. Though people praise us, always look on such praise as a great danger, for thus it is to men who have renounced all things."

"We are like innocent lambs under the crook of a shepherd boy," Guy told his father. "Isn't it a marvelous thing that men so used to camp life or idle jousts and tournaments should come together like this? Bernard is like a mother to us all, feeding us on the love of God."

From Bernard himself Tescelin learned other pleasant things about the company. "For all these men," he reported, "silence is the rule—not a sad silence, but such as angels keep."

"That I know well," Tescelin answered. "For it is by silence that holy men communicate with one another, even faster and more vividly than they could by using human language—and, be it said, more sublimely."

"Silence unites our souls to God, feeds our minds," Bernard added. "Only in silence can a man develop a taste for spiritual things. By it a man's senses are cleansed—his eyes purified, his hearing washed of noise, and his feelings refined to heed the slightest touch of grace."

With great surprise the townspeople and country folk watched what was happening at Fontaines Castle. "Can Bernard and his followers really be planning to throw their lives away in such a fashion?" they asked.

The little company turned its attention more

and more to future plans. "Are we to join one of the great Orders already established in the Church," the men wondered, "or will Bernard found a new one?"

Having studied the matter for a long time, Bernard answered their queries. "I think it better that we enter a community founded already, perhaps the monks at Citeaux. There the ancient Rule of St. Benedict is observed with full rigor and purity."

Some of the younger men shuddered at hearing these words. "Citeaux is one of the most severe monasteries in the Church," they exclaimed. "Even holy people are frightened by it and pity the monks who go there."

"All of us know something about the great Abbey of Cluny," Bernard explained gently. "Such a powerful, wealthy monastery cannot be for us. The religious life there seems to be fading gradually away, but the Benedictine spirit springs into fresh life in such places as Citeaux. There, I think, can we become true monks and find the solitude and peace of God that all of us seek."

"I've heard one of the Abbots of Citeaux changed the customary black habit to one of a grayish white," one of the company said. "At the monastery the monks keep strict silence day and night, spending their lives in a round of work and prayer, and are concerned only with thoughts of God."

"The Cistercian Order exists for penance, contemplation, and the chanting of the Divine Office," added another of the company. "The work of preaching and teaching, indeed no pastoral duties at all do they perform."

Well versed in affairs all over Burgundy, Guido now supplied more information to the listening company. "Citeaux has become a standing rebuke to the Abbey of Cluny and to other relaxed monasteries. Stephen Harding, the Abbot of Citeaux, has much to suffer from the envy and accusations of less virtuous monks. Why, people are even saying that Citeaux is upsetting the peace, that it's throwing the whole monastic system out of gear!"

"And it almost looks as if they're right," somebody exclaimed. "The monastery has only a small number of sickly monks, and the Abbot himself fears that the Order will soon perish for lack of members."

At Citeaux, meanwhile, only a few miles from the town of Dijon, Abbot Stephen had grown so desperate that he rushed one day to the bedside of a dying monk. "I command you in virtue of holy obedience," he cried out, "that you return after death, if God wills, to tell us what we should believe about the life we're trying to lead here."

The dying man whispered his reply. "I willingly shall do what you command, on condition that you pray I receive the grace to obey."

Some days after the monk had been buried, Abbot Stephen knelt alone in the forest, his cowl over his head, when suddenly the dead man appeared to him in vision, resplendent with light.

"How does it fare with you, good soul?" Stephen asked fearfully.

"I am happy," replied the shade, "and have only come back to obey your command. Know, then, that the way of life practiced at Citeaux much pleases Our Lord. Behold, God will shortly reveal His mercy and send so many persons to the monastery that they'll overflow the building and swarm from it like bees from a hive, filling the whole world."

With these words, the vision disappeared and the Abbot hurried to tell his monks the good news. One of the monks then revealed a dream he had not spoken of before. "I saw a huge army of men coming to wash their clothes in the stream near our gates. Then a voice said the stream should be named Enon, after the place where St. John baptized the Lord Jesus Christ."

"Evidently God means us to know that many will join Citeaux to wash their souls clean by prayer and penance," the Abbot told his handful of monks.

The first step toward fulfillment of these dreams and portents was now approaching realization, for Bernard and his little company of followers had decided to apply for entry to the monastery of Citeaux. "Go, now, each of you," Bernard told his men, "and settle affairs with your families. My brothers and I will gather at Fontaines to ask Lord Tescelin's blessing on our venture."

With Nivard and Humbeline at his side, Tescelin received his five sons with tears in his eyes. "Surely a man can suffer as I do but once in a lifetime!" he said, embracing each of his sons in turn. "I am to lose nearly all my sons at one blow, and the comforts of old age will not be mine." Grieving, but accepting the will of God, good Tescelin bowed his head in his hands. As Bernard and his brothers packed their few belongings, Nivard and Humbeline ran from one older brother to the other, whimpering and tugging at their tunics.

"Do not weep, little ones," Bernard told the youngsters. "You shall be our father's comfort now, so you must be brave in facing whatever the future holds." With golden words that came so easily to him, Bernard soothed his father, too, as best he might. "Surely you know that God demands that home and parents be sacrificed when He calls," he said gently. "Did not Christ say that everyone who leaves house or brethren or sisters or father or mother or wife or children or lands for His sake would receive a hundredfold and possess life everlasting?"

Lord Tescelin's firm faith in these truths led him to accept his sons' vocation without further complaint. As the travelers assembled in the castle courtyard, their skimpy packs on their backs, the eldest son Guido, Tescelin's legal heir, turned to young Nivard. "Adieu, my little brother," he said as he pointed toward the castle with its surrounding forests and fields. "Soon you will have all our estates, Fontaines and all its lands, for your very own."

Nivard's eyes glinted with tears. "What! Will you take heaven as your inheritance and leave only the earth for me? The trade isn't fair!" At these words the boy rushed to his father, crying, "Let me go with my brothers, my lord. God calls me, too, to follow where they go."

Knowing the boy was quite old enough to choose, Tescelin gave his assent, and after a short delay for packing, Nivard joined his brothers at the castle gate. The last good-bys were said: then Tescelin and Humbeline stood at the drawbridge watching Bernard and the others ride slowly away over the sun-baked road.

3

With those who joined him at Chatillon, Bernard counted thirty noblemen in the party bound for Citeaux, all with but one desire—to become holy monks. Along the way he explained something of manastic history to the young Nivard, who listened eagerly. "It was St. Benedict in the sixth century who began to found monasteries in the western Church. His first Abbey was built on the heights of Monte Cassino, south of Rome, and since then almost all monasteries have followed the Rule of life he laid down."

"But the Abbey of Citeaux is hardly as old as I am," Nivard exclaimed.

Bernard laughed. "Citeaux came into being only fifteen years ago. But be patient now, for as soon as we arrive there you'll learn all there is to know about it."

After a journey of two or three days, the little company, dusty and travel-worn, arrived at the monastery gates, where all prostrated before the Abbot Stephen, who came out to greet them. The wonder-stricken man would never forget that year of 1113.

Learning that the thirty men had come to join the faltering Abbey, Stephen at once intoned the *Te Deum,* in which the travelers and the few bedraggled Cistercians joined. Within a few days Bernard, his brothers, and the other noblemen received the Cistercian garb from the Abbot's hands and began their novitiate, a period of formation before pronouncing their vows. Thus, when he was only twenty-three years old, did Bernard's life as a Cistercian monk begin.

"Tell me," Stephen asked the thirty new

arrivals one day, "why did you choose poor Cîteaux?"

Speaking for all, Bernard answered, "Because we want to live unknown and forgotten. Because we want to die to everything except Christ and His Cross."

As the weeks and months progressed, Abbot Stephen could not help but voice his surprise at Bernard's swift progress. "His virtue astonishes me," Stephen told his Prior. "Young Bernard keeps the Holy Rule as if his very life depended on it."

"And so it does," murmured the Prior.

"Well you know," Stephen continued, "that Bernard's too weak to cut trees or to do other heavy work our monks perform. Yet he insists on trying and sometimes rivals even the strongest men in what he accomplishes."

The Prior, who directed the novices, had more observations to make. "For Bernard the things of the body hardly seem to exist! It's almost as if he sees without seeing, hears without hearing, eats without tasting. The other day I watched him drink some oil when he thought

[42]

he'd poured water in his cup. I'm sure Bernard doesn't know yet whether there's a roof on the chapel or not, he's so recollected, though he prays there half the night."

Responding to every touch of grace, Bernard grew more and more sensitive to even the slightest imperfections. He had promised, for example, to recite the Penitential Psalms every night for the repose of his mother's soul, but he forgot to do so one evening.

The Abbot, who happened to notice this omission, gently chided him about it. "Brother Bernard, to whom did you assign reciting the seven psalms last night?" asked Stephen.

"To no one, my lord," Bernard admitted, regretting his lapse of memory. "Give me a penance, good Father, and grant me your pardon."

When relatives happened to stop at the monastery one day to visit Bernard and his brothers, he took such keen interest in their chatter that his peace of soul was afterward disturbed. "I feel the bad effects of my dissipation," he confessed to the Abbot, "and even my prayers give me little consolation. I beg you, Father, absolve me so that grace may return."

Every tendency of weak human nature the young man strove to overcome, as the Prior's reports to the Abbot made plain. "I'm afraid Bernard's ascetical practices are weakening his health," the Prior pointed out. "His stomach can hardly hold food anymore, and he's so thin that the light nearly shines through his body. Yet he's so desperately eager to follow the Rule, and who am I to dissuade him!"

"He grieves when we don't allow him to chop wood or help reap the grain," Stephen remarked, "yet I know such work is much too heavy for him."

Actually, Bernard had great love for the good, beautiful earth God created for mankind. "It is principally in the fields and woods," he declared, "that I learn to contemplate heavenly things and to pray. Under the trees or in the warm sun I can meditate very easily on the truths of Holy Scripture. Really, I wonder if I've not learned more from the beech trees and the oaks than from any schoolmaster!" The secret of

Bernard's wisdom was the grace of God, his devotion to prayer, his profound meditation on the teachings of the Church.

A year after they entered Citeaux, the novitiate training ended, and in April Bernard and his thirty companions took their vows as Cistercian monks. By solemnly promising to live poor, chaste, and obedient, these noblemen stripped themselves of everything the world holds dear.

Tescelin, who attended the vow-taking ceremonies, looked aghast at Bernard's appearance. "The boy is thin and pale," the lord reported after his return to Fontaines, "his body almost worn away with penances. He's fasted so rigorously that he can hardly eat solid foods anymore. Yet the Abbot tells me that he never complains or seeks exceptions to the Rule." Even as Tescelin worried, though, he recalled what Bernard had said: "Did a monk but realize how great his obligations are, he would not eat one morsel of bread without first watering it with his tears!"

Though he practiced poverty with great strictness, Bernard had no use for dirty cells, dirty habits, or other carelessness. "Such is a mark of sloth or affection," he said. Times of prayer and meditation seemed only too short for him. Though silence suited him best, he did not neglect speaking when the good of his neighbor demanded, for as a good religious he became all things to all men. Noble and common folk, learned or ignorant, the rich and poor—all benefited from the grace and fire of his words.

It was Bernard's presence at Citeaux that spurred the monastery's growth. So many flocked to join the monks as the years passed that Abbot Stephen began to found branch houses elsewhere in Burgundy, then in other provinces. The Abbey of La Ferte, then the Abbey of Pontigny, became Citeaux's first two daughter monasteries. When Hugh, the Earl of Troyes, offered extensive grounds on his estates for a third monastery, three years after Bernard joined Citeaux, the Abbot Stephen determined upon a far-reaching step.

"I shall make Bernard an abbot," he told his councilors, "give him the crosier, and send him with twelve monks to found a monastery on the Earl of Troyes' lands. We lack money for this, of course, but God will provide. Bernard, his five brothers, his cousin Robert, and six other monks will accompany him."

Arrangements for the new foundation proceeded quickly, and in a few weeks Bernard, now an ordained priest as well as abbot, and the twelve, chanting the required itinerary prayers, marched away from their beloved Citeaux. None of the white-clad figures turned back for a last look, so obedient had they grown.

The journey took the little company to a sunny valley in the Langres plateau on the borders of Burgundy and Champagne. After a few days' march through wild, empty hills they arrived in a sunny valley surrounded on all sides by forest. It was June 25, 1115.

"This place, I've heard, is called Vallee d'Absinth, or the Valley of Wormwood," said one of the monks.

"We'll call it Clairvaux," Bernard said, "for from this valley will shine forth to all the world the sunshine of holy lives."

"Clairvaux—the Valley of Light," Nivard murmured into his cowl. "What a beautiful name!" From this time on the names of Bernard and Clairvaux became inseparable: to think of one is to think of the other. Because of its Abbot, of the saints who lived there, and the God the monks there served, the fame of Clairvaux will never die.

But Bernard and his twelve monks had little time to ponder such things. As soon as they arrived, they set to with knives and axes to clear enough land on which they built small wooden shelters. The country folk of Langres rejoiced in having good monks settle in their midst and gathered to help the tiny community get off to a good start. Soon as there were roofs overhead, Bernard summoned his monks to an assembly.

"I appoint Gerard and Guy as the monastery cellarers; they will look after temporal affairs. Andrew shall be the porter, looking after the care of those who ask hospitality at our doors. To-morrow, my brothers, I shall go to the Bishop in Chalons to ask his blessing on our venture and be confirmed as Abbot."

On Bernard's appearance next day in the see city, Bishop William of Champeaux felt quite shocked as he glimpsed the Abbot's worn face.

"How can a twenty-five-year-old man be so emaciated," he exclaimed to his attendants. "Death itself seems painted on his face."

Convinced that the humble Cistercian was quite mad, the courtiers hid their mocking smiles from their Bishop's sharp eyes. "Lord William will have nothing to do with this beggar," they whispered, nudging one another.

But the court gasped as William strode from the dais to embrace Abbot Bernard and lead him to sit at his right hand, alongside the episcopal throne.

"I see in this man," the bishop mused, "a true *servum Dei,* a real servant of God, predestined for great things."

The approval so plainly manifested by their bishop impressed the bystanders. "If the great William befriends these poor Cistercian monks," they agreed, "we are not to scorn them!"

His affairs settled with Bishop William, Abbot Bernard returned to Clairvaux to rejoin his subjects, who as the months passed worked from dawn to dusk to clear patches of land for sowing.

From the scanty supplies of grain they had on hand they made coarse bread of barley flour, and for vegetables they ate vetches, cockle, or pea plants. Sometimes they boiled beech tree leaves, serving these because they lacked other edible herbs.

"Only with hard labor and sweat do we gather a few handfuls of barley and millet," Guy reported to Bernard. "Out of this meager supply comes a batch of loaves now and then, but there is little else for the monastery's needs."

"A mere dozen hands are not enough to build, plow, remove rocks, drain the swampy places, and grow crops sufficient to supply our table," Gerard told his older brother, who knew these facts only too well.

"God will provide, good brother," the latter replied. "Do not trouble Bernard with these matters. Let us remain faithful to our long hours of prayer. Keep the Rule, good brother, and the Rule will keep you!"

"I fear that now the novelty of our monastery has worn off, " said Gerard, "we can expect less and less help from the country folk. Do you realize, Guy, that our very salt supply has been exhausted for days! Men will die unless there's a pinch of salt now and then."

"Something does have to be done at once," Bernard agreed when informed of the dire poverty and distress facing his community.

Summoning the monk Guibert, the Abbot gave his instructions. "Go, my son, into the town to buy some salt at the market."

"At once, good Father. May I have some money to pay for it?"

"Of money there is none, but have confidence. There is One above who keeps my purse, Who looks after all my treasures."

"But, Father, if I go empty-handed, I fear I'll return empty-handed!" Guibert not only had a literal mind, but common sense told him as much.

"Go! Go with confidence!" Bernard smiled his dismissal. "I repeat—my treasurer will accompany you on the road; will give you the means to buy what we need."

In puzzled silence, Guibert trugged over the winding road to Challons, mulling over his Abbot's cryptic words. Just before he reached the walls, a priest stopped to inquire from whence Guibert came.

Pouring out the sad state of affairs at Clairvaux to the stranger, Guibert had no more than ended his recital than the priest led him personally to the marketplace and ordered as many provisions loaded into Guibert's cart as it would hold. As the priest paid the shopkeepers, Guibert thanked him for all the Cistercians at Clairvaux, and dragging the little cart along, returned to the monastery.

"I told you, my son," Abbot Bernard exclaimed to the smiling monk, "that God would look after us. There is nothing more necessary for the Christian than complete confidence in Him. Never fail to trust, and your life will be happy."

Such assistance could only stave off temporarily the extreme hardships facing Clairvaux, until some of the less hardy monks could not contain their misgivings. ·

"Had we not best return to Citeaux?" they asked Bernard. "Plainly, we have made no progress in this valley, and none can be expected in the future."

Abbot Bernard refused to let discouraging prospects overwhelm either himself or his men. Through the severe winter he fought to keep his monastery alive no matter what trials beset it. Begging God one day to have mercy, the Abbot heard a voice sounding through the chapel: "Arise, Bernard," it said, "your prayer is heard!"

Within days the fortunes of Clairvaux began to improve noticeably as people from country and town beat a path to the monastery doors with offers of wood, grain, and other desperately needed supplies. As these gifts piled up, Bernard cried out one day, "Too much abundance is worse than famine!" He feared for the strict poverty the Cistercians were bound to observe.

A man of iron regarding his own penances, the Abbot of Clairvaux demanded a great deal from the monks in his charge. One of the weaker members finally voiced his objections. "Good Father Abbot, you are so severe on the smallest distractions, the tiniest faults, that it depresses me to confess or to accuse myself in Chapter."

Having considered this monition, Bernard at once recognized the justice of it. As a punishment he left off preaching to his monks for some days, but grace inspired him to resume the talks that all his monks found so beneficial.

As time went on, grants of pasture and forest land were made to the Clairvaux monks. The lay brothers who joined the community turned these into productive farm lands that gradually made the monastery self-supporting. As the cellarers Guy and Gerard grew in experience and skill, the temporal affairs of the house caused less concern for the hard-pressed monks. They, of course, shared their abundance with the poor; they taught farming methods, reclaimed swamps, and showed how poor fields could be improved.

"It is their sweat that fertilizes the land," the people said. "Our whole lives now seem to revolve around Clairvaux. How true it is that only the Church brings good order, civilization, and culture to society."

4

To the one hundred and thirty monks who had by now joined Clairvaux, the Abbot Bernard was the spiritual, guide and father. The burden of directing them, added to his extreme penances, undermined his health so much that his friend, Bishop William, feared the saint might die.

To the first General Chapter of the Cistercian Order that had been summoned at the Abbey of Citeaux in 1116, the Bishop hurried with an unusual request.

"Put Abbot Bernard in my charge for one year," William begged the chapter members, "for the man's killing himself with extreme mortifications. I'm told that he eats so little that now he can hardly bear the sight of food. He must have more rest and take better care of his health."

The Chapter agreeing to the Bishop's request, William ordered Bernard to occupy a cell away from the others, a kind of infirmary where he would be left in peace, and then hired a country doctor to attend him.

Actually, Bishop William seemed rather horrified by what he found at Clairvaux. "The monks' bread seems made of mud rather than flour," he remarked to his priests. "Whatever taste their food has comes only from hunger, yet the novices find it too dainty."

A friend visited Bernard one day and could not check his remonstrances. "Why, good Bernard, you live in a cell no better than a leper's dugout by the roadside. And your quack of a doctor—how do you put up with him?"

Bernard smiled. "Consider this, my friend. Before I came here, reasonable men obeyed me; but now, by a just judgment of God, I must obey a man without reason."

The year of isolation finally passed, Bernard's strength returned, and he resumed his abbatial duties in the monastery, including the regular sermons he preached to his monks, sermons so wonderful that the whole world seemed to be talking about them.

One day Tescelin himself appeared at the gates, begging admission to Clairvaux. The Abbot clothed his venerable old father in cowl and habit as all the sons of Fontaines Castle stood by, weeping with joy. Within a year or so, the good Tescelin died at Clairvaux, an event crowning a long life of manly service to the Lord Christ he had served so well.

Between the years 1118 and 1121, Bernard began the first monastic foundations stemming from the Abbey of Clairvaux, these first three houses being Trois Fontaines, Fontenay, and Foigny. Preoccupied as he was with their establishment, Bernard failed to notice that his cousin, the monk Robert, who had followed Bernard to Citeaux as a mere lad of fourteen years, was growing most dissatisfied with the Cistercian way of life.

"Why don't you come with us to Cluny?" asked certain visitors from that Abbey. "We have heard that your parents years ago promised to send you there."

Robert listened eagerly to the temptors, then without permission wrote to Rome to gain approval for the change. When the message at last arrived, the young monk stole away one night from Clairvaux to join the monks at Cluny.

"If you have left us to lead a more perfect life, well and good," Bernard wrote him soon afterward. "But if not, blush and tremble. If warm and comfortable furs, if fine and precious cloths, if long sleeves and ample hoods, if dainty coverlets and soft woolen shirts make a saint, why do I delay and not follow you at once? But these things are comforts for the weak, not the arms of fighting men. The soul is not fattened out of frying pans."

The longest of all Bernard's letters went to

persuade Robert, yet it had no immediate effect. Though Robert knew perfectly well that his parents' arrangement with Cluny had no binding force, he remained there for four years, until the Abbot himself ordered his return to Clairvaux, along with several other Cluniac monks.

As more and more Cistercian monasteries sprang up in Burgundy and elsewhere in France, the young Abbot Bernard, not yet thirty years old, became one of the most influential figures in the Order. "Truly he is the oracle sent by God," the elders and abbots admitted, "and much good will come to the Church because he has revived the true monastic spirit all over Europe!"

"Abbot Bernard's cell has become a kind of lighthouse in these troubled times," one abbot said. "From it wisdom and light radiate through the entire Church. Whose writings, sermons, and teaching have attracted greater attention? Who can count the visitors who stream to Clairvaux week after week?"

"But my cares leave me no time, give me no rest," Bernard complained mildly. "Yet a man must sacrifice beloved solitude when a neighbor's welfare is at stake. That's better than following one's own desires for peace and quiet."

"How can you, Bernard," asked a monk one day, "be so hard on wrongdoers and those who treat others unjustly?"

"If the enemies of holiness and justice have hard heads," Bernard explained, "then ours must be harder still in righting the wrong. After all, only a diamond will cut a diamond."

Even to bishops and other dignitaries the young Abbot did not mince his words. "You may imagine," he told one rich priest, "that what belongs to the Church belongs to you because you officiate there, but you are mistaken. Even though a man who serves the altar should live by the altar, he must not use church goods to further luxury or pride. Whatever you take that doesn't go simply for bare nourishment and plain, simple clothing is stealing and sacrilege."

By letter, messenger, or in person, the nobles and Church leaders and ordinary folk sought Bernard's wise counsel, for everyone recognized that what Bernard said was usually right.

"Nobody's too humble for his attention," said the poor who sought him out.

"Not even the greatest princes make him afraid," said the barons.

The most wayward sinners are not too miserable for his helping hand," said the outcasts.

It seemed that everywhere the Abbot Bernard went there were miracles to mark the journey, far too many to recount. Crowds followed him out of the towns, begging his blessing; crippled and sick men, and men possessed by the devil cried out to Bernard as he passed.

At the Abbey of Foigny, where he came for dedication of the church, a strange story unfolded. "The ceremonies had to be stopped," Bernard heard, "because hundreds of thousands of flies have invaded the building, and there's no way to drive them out."

As Bernard looked through the church portals, his ears buzzed with the sound of the frenzied flies. All at once, in loud, ringing tones, he cried out: *"Excommunicabo eas! Excommunicabo eas!"*

A murmur went through the crowd assembled in the square, but Abbot Bernard left the scene without a word. Next morning as the townspeople assembled, they found the church floor covered with a layer of dead flies so thick that men had to remove them with shovels.

An example of his miraculous influence on souls occurred some weeks later at Clairvaux, when a group of German knights on their way to a tournament stopped there for a night's lodging. These young noblemen passionately loved the combats of chivalry and spoke of nothing but lists, tilts, and tournaments.

"But how can you attend such things during the holy season of Lent, two weeks of it already gone?" Bernard asked. "I beg you, try to avoid such amusements for a while."

Much too proud and vain, the cavaliers refused to consider it.

"In that case," said the Abbot, "I'll ask God to grant this favor," and he beckoned to the guestmaster. "Bring the visitors wine," and this carried in, he turned to the guests. "Here is the wine of Clairvaux! Now drink—to your souls'

[62]

health."

Early next morning the troupe rode gaily away from the monastery's stern walls, yet as the sun rose higher, the spirits of the light-hearted company sank lower and lower.

"What can be wrong?" one asked to break the long silence.

"My conscience prickles me like a hairshirt," said another.

"I think that what we've seen at Clairvaux has made us uneasy," put in a third.

Pondering, the knights cantered along for an hour or two, but suddenly all wheeled their horses, as if at a shouted command, and galloped back to the monastery.

"We are stung to the heart by our vain lives," the young nobles admitted to Bernard. "Here, take our armor and lances, our rich clothes, and let us wear the poor garb of monks."

In this determination the little band persevered, and all eventually pronounced their Cistercian vows.

En route to one of his monasteries one day, Bernard stopped to visit his friends, the Carthusians at La Trappe, where he arrived on a brightly caparisoned horse and followed by a brilliantly clad train.

"How can the famous Abbot of Clairvaux, poor as a church mouse, square this display of luxury with his vow of poverty," muttered one Carthusian as he watched the retinue approach.

Hearing of the criticism, Bernard ordered an attendant to bring his horse, which still wore the jingling harness and ornate saddle.

"Why, I've never noticed the bridle and saddle before," Bernard said as he strode by the beast. "I simply took the mount loaned to me by a monk of Cluny, harness and all!"

The lords and ladies who insisted on trailing Bernard all over France accounted for the Abbot's brilliant train. Their apparel, after all, was their own affair.

Around the year 1123 a serious drought brought famine to Burgundy and other French domains, with the Abbey of Clairvaux and other Cistercian monasteries taking the lead to relieve it.

"God seems to make them a kind of Egypt,"

the grateful people exclaimed, bearing away the bulging packs given them by the monks, whose farming methods, irrigation canals, and carefully preserved harvests prevented the disaster. "Look how Bernard, like Joseph of old, feeds an entire country. Think of the three thousand men now being cared for by the monks until rain falls again on their dry fields!"

Worn out by these added labors, Bernard once again fell seriously ill, and as he lay tossing feverishly from side to side, he saw in his mind's eye the devil accusing him before the throne of God.

To the devil's charges, Bernard made only one answer. "I confess that I'm unworthy of the glory of heaven," he said, "and that I cannot get there on my own merits. But the Lord Jesus Christ has purchased heaven with His Precious Blood and transferred title of it on me. Thus, through His adorable Passion and His mercy, I hope to obtain it."

The chain of monasteries springing up during these years had untold influence on European civilization and culture. Whole towns grew up near them and orchards and farms made a complex pattern of groves and fields outside their walls. Only because of the monasteries did the continent emerge from what historians call the Dark Ages.

Not only did the religious houses serve as schools, hostels, hospitals, and orphanages, but they became houses of correction. All the works of mercy, including those for wrongdoers, were dear to Bernard's heart. Traveling one day to see the Count of Champagne, he met a procession leading a prisoner to execution. Forcing his way into the throng, the holy Abbot clutched the leash on which the poor fellow was being dragged along. "Trust this man to me," Bernard cried, "for I wish to hang him with my own hands."

"Bernard hang a man! Unthinkable!" The crowd gasped with surprise at the saint's words.

At the palace, the Count greeted Abbot Bernard with consternation.

"Alas, Reverend Father, what are you doing? The wretch you bring here has damned himself a thousand times, yet you come to plead for him!

Would you save the devil?"

"No, prince, I do not ask you to leave the man go unpunished," the Abbot replied. "On the contrary! You demand he expiate his crime by immediate execution, but I say let his punishment last as long as he lives! Let the Cross be his torment, the long penance for his misdeeds."

With that, Bernard laid his own tunic over the half-naked malefactor and bore him off to Clairvaux. There the wolf became a lamb and lived as a gentle monk for thirty years until his death.

By the year 1124, Bernard's sister Humbeline had become a grand, worldly lady who with her husband moved in the highest circles of twelfth-century society. Longing to see her brothers again, she journeyed to Clairvaux in company with a band of merry, noisy friends who arrived at the gates singing and shouting. The uproar brought Bernard to his cell window, from which he spied his sister, but he refused to come down to visit her.

The icy reception stunned Humbeline into serious reflection. "I know, I'm a sinner," she told her other brothers, "but did not Our Lord die for such as I? Tell the good Bernard that if he despises my rich clothes and flighty manners, he should not spurn my soul! Let him receive me, and I will do whatever he commands."

The kind Bernard could not refuse his sister for long, and in his talks with her during the following days he proved once more to be the channel of grace to the last of Tescelin's children. With a rule of life Bernard gave her, Humbeline left the monastery to return home, where her virtue soon rivaled her mother's. On her husband's death, Bernard's sister entered a convent to spend the rest of her life in devoted service to God.

5

The twelfth century marked the end of one age and the dawn of a new one: feudalism was ready to fall apart, towns and cities were growing in size and independence, and the age of cathedrals and great universities was at hand. Though Bernard sought his Lord in poverty, silence, and solitude at Clairvaux, his gifts of mind and soul could not be ignored by the world at large. By the time the first quarter of the twelfth century passed, the world began coming to Bernard, and Bernard himself went to meet that world.

"He's a saint, he works miracles!" said people everywhere. "He's a theologian, a man whose wisdom is more than a matter of books and schooling," said the Church leaders.

As his reputation spread, princes and bishops sought his advice; even the Holy See brought him problems for settlement. One of the Cardinals urged him to write a book on the love of God; the Bishop of Sens asked him to compose a treatise on the spiritual life for bishops.

"Who are we that we should write for bishops!" exclaimed Bernard at this request, "yet who are we that w eshould not obey."

More than once vacant sees were offered him, but Bernard refused them all, even appealing to Rome to prevent his forcible consecration.

His opposition to the election of unworthy men to bishoprics and other ecclesiastical dignities earned Bernard many enemies who sought by slander and invective to damage his growing reputation.

"A monk ought to confine himself to his

cloister," said these opponents, angry that Bernard should wield such influence.

Fearlessly, Bernard answered that monks were soldiers of Christ just as other Christians were. "Monks, too," he said, "ought to defend the truth and the honor of God's Church."

In the year 1127 a visitor came to Clairvaux with good news. "You know, of course," he told Bernard, "that the Bishop of Paris, Stephen de Senlis, has determined to follow your good advice. Though he's one of the king's most trusted councilors and a leader of France, the bishop has decided to give up his life at court so that all his time may be spent caring for his episcopal see."

"And King Louis' friendship for Stephen— a fact that all Paris marveled to see—has now turned to violent hatred. Yes, I've heard the story," Bernard said, his voice troubled.

"The kings displeasure has been aggravated, indeed," said the visitor, "by certain priests of the city who are annoyed by the strict discipline Bishop Stephen has imposed on them. Their false reports and intrigues have made the king angrier than ever with his former good friend.

In fact, the king has lately confiscated all the bishop's property!"

"Property, of course, that belongs to the Church!" Bernard put in.

In Paris meanwhile, Bishop Stephen fought fearlessly against the encroachments of the state upon the Church. "Since threats and remonstrances avail nothing, let it be known that I place the King of France under interdict!"

Interdict meant banishment from the Mass, from the Sacraments, from all the Church's avenues of grace. "Perhaps this most serious of punishments will bring the king back in line," Stephen said as he left the city to visit Citeaux, where a Chapter of the Cistercian Order had gathered.

Arrived at the famous monastery, Stephen addressed the assembly as soon as possible. "I have come to ask your protection—you, the Abbots, who must use all your spiritual forces to prevent harm to the Church."

Members of the Chapter studied thoroughly the situation in Paris and directed Abbot Bernard to write the French king.

"Threaten anathema! Tell the king that we shall appeal to the pope!" The Chapter delegates agreed unanimously that the rightful authority of the Church must be safeguarded at all costs.

With Bernard's letter in hand, the French king confronted his council. "Make peace with your bishop," the members advised, "for your subjects are growing restless under the interdict, and your very crown may be endangered."

An appeal to the pope and a promise to return the confiscated property seemed to settle the affair. "But there are other ways to get even with Stephen," said Louis, who began persecuting the Church less openly after the interdict was lifted.

Watching the course of events closely, the Abbot Bernard felt the interdict had been removed without due cause, and he minced no words in writing his remonstrances to the pontiff. "The honor of the Church has been sacrificed because of Your Holiness' action in the Paris affair. By humility and firmness Bishop Stephen had begun to soothe the king's anger, but now the authority of the Sovereign Pontiff apparently makes the king bolder than ever in coveting what belongs to the Church alone."

Nor was the King of France too exalted a personage to be spared Bernard's grave warnings. "If you continue in this evil business," the saint wrote him, "then expect the chastisement which your crimes deserve. Behold, your eldest son, though he is a young man, will die, though he is heir of the kingdom!"

Two years later this prediction came true, as Prince Philip, a lad only sixteen years old, was riding one day outside the Paris walls. A grunting little pig scuttled into the road, so suddenly that the prince's horse reared and tossed his noble rider from the saddle and then toppled over on the boy. At once Philip's attendants freed him, carried him into a nearby house, and summoned the doctors. But nothing could be done. At night fall, the prince of France died, his death marked by tolling bells and fear-marked faces.

More than anyone else King Louis mourned his son. "Now, too late, I repent my greed and ambition. Let Stephen be in peace," he ordered his courtiers, "and let us no more war against the authority of the men of God."

For Abbot Bernard the settlement brought only one less call on his energies. Day after day he worked to establish monastic reforms, to make new foundations in France and other countries. "I love solitude, yearn for nothing but the walls of my cell," he cried, "yet I must travel the roads of the world, take part in the affairs of kings, bishops, and popes! Will there ever be an end!"

One of King Louis' sons, the Prince Henry, now decided to visit Clairvaux, the monastery he had heard so much about. What he observed among the Cistercians there so affected the prince that he hurried to announce an important decision to Abbot Bernard: "I will never quit this place again, Father. Allow me to dismiss my knights and squires that I may stay and become a good monk like all the other men here."

Knowing the prince, like so many other noblemen through the years, had a true vocation to the Cistercian life, Bernard allowed him to remain at Clairvaux. The weeks and months passed, yet the prince survived every trial, every test, placed in his way.

"We've made him cook, carry wood, scrub floors," the novice-master reported to the Abbot, "yet Prince Henry continues to be one of the humblest monks in the monastery."

Another lad of royal blood, Amadeus, a near relative of the German emperor, also discarded the insignia of royalty to bury himself for the rest of his life at Clairvaux. Thus, indeed, did there come hundreds of other men, highborn or low, to follow Bernard as Cistercian monks.

In the year 1128, Pope Honorius summoned Bernard to the Council at Troyes, a gathering of French prelates held to discuss problems facing the Church throughout the land. Bernard, whose taste for the world's important affairs had not improved despite his involvement in so many of them, tried once more to make his position clear to the authorities.

"I am decided never again to leave my solitude," he informed the Council members, "or to undertake affairs not befitting my vocation."

The Cardinal Bishop of Bergamo, the pope's

legate at the Council, remonstrated with the reluctant Abbot, but Bernard had his excuses ready.

"I was ready to obey you," he wrote the cardinal, "but my body could not follow my spirit, being burnt even now by fever. Let my friends judge if this reason be sufficient. It is these very friends who use the obedience I've vowed to my superiors to drag me time and again from the cloister and to plunge me back into the world. If the business of the Council is so important, why, indeed, look for my help? The work you want me to do is either easy or hard. If it's easy, then it can be done very well without me. If it's hard, then my poor talents will avail little. Nevertheless, I declare to you, Reverend Father, that difficult though the task may be, I will submit without murmur to the orders you might choose to give me. I leave it to your discretion, however, to spare my weakness."

Unswayed by Bernard's pleas, the cardinal prelate commanded the Abbot to join with the other leading churchmen at the Council. At this meeting Bernard's assistance helped in forming and issuing various regulations governing the clergy in France.

"Our work has been done," the cardinal told the assemblage afterward, but news has reached me that will require more sittings. As you all know, there are groups of men today who try to live like monks and soldiers both. The Knights of Malta, or Hospitalers, came into existence shortly after the First Crusade to care for the sick and to protect the thousands of pilgrims traveling to the Holy Land and in the country itself. A few years ago, several French knights joined Godfrey de Bouillon in Jerusalem into a society meant to guard the road, to guide pilgrims on their way, and, of course, to fight the infidel hordes that surround the cities in Palestine that the French now control."

"That group is called the Templars, is it not?" asked one of the members of the Council.

"So it is," the cardinal agreed. "Because the crusaders occupied a house believed to stand on the site of Solomon's temple. The group has only nine or ten members now—all living in common, subject to military law, and obedience to their Grand Master, Hugh de Paganis. His Holiness the Pope now directs you, the Council of Troyes, to give the Templars a definite form and a set of rules."

There now rose before the assembly the Grand Master himself to unfold the purpose of the newly established order. "We believe," he said, "that the Church has bulwarks enough against her spiritual foes, but she needs protection against her human enemies, particularly in the East. There, as you know well, the Mohammedans stand ready to cut off all access to the Holy Sepulcher and the other shrines. The Templars believe we can help safeguard the Church against these infidels. Indeed, the time may come when the whole world will benefit from our mission."

The Council applauded the Grand Master and set about their deliberations. "Draw up statutes for the organization," its leaders ordered Bernard, an order the great Abbot immediately obeyed.

Once the Templars' Rule had been drawn up and approved by the Council, Bernard wrote a tract clarifying the role of these unique men. "The obedience of the Knights Templar," he explained, "is such that no one acts except at his superior's orders. From their leader the knights receive food and clothing, for all live like poor men, with no personal property. Without wife or children, the knights live in common and work busily even when not at war. Every fault against discipline merits severe punishment, even light words or immoderate laughter. The Templars forbid hunting, singing vain songs, playing dice, chess games, and other worldly entertainments. When a battle approaches, they go forth clad in ungilt iron armor, the men's hearts burning with faith in God! Like bold lions they fall on the infidel armies, fearing neither Islam's hordes nor Islam's diabolical cruelty."

As his work at Troyes drew to a close, the Abbot Bernard felt more poignantly than ever his long absence from beloved Clairvaux. "Have pity on me, have pity on me!" he wrote the monks there, "you who have the blessing to serve God in an inviolable sanctuary, far from the tumult of business. As for me, wretch that I am, condemned to continual labors, I am like a little unfledged bird, almost always out of its nest and exposed to violence and storm."

The Cistercian Rule forbade monks to wander from their cells to preach or teach, and only because duty and charity demanded it did Bernard leave his place at Clairvaux. "It is the duty of a religious man to weep," he said, "not to teach. Cities must be to him like prisons, and solitude must be his heaven. What can one think of the monk, however, who finds solitude a prison and cities his paradise?"

Bernard had learned well the secrets of heaven, the science of the saints. Better than any of his monks he knew that the best school of holiness was found in solitude, penance, and contemplation. Though he was forced oftentimes to mix with crowds or become involved in affairs of church and state, he never lost his recollection and absorption in God. So deeply could he lose himself in God that his monks one day found him walking by a lakeshore without his realizing there was a body of water anywhere near.

6

As the regulations drawn up at the Council of Troyes affected the conduct of monks and diocesan priests, certain worldly clergymen found the new rules terribly burdensome.

"Bernard, the monk of Clairvaux, must take the blame for the restrictions being laid on us," these men complained. "Let us appeal to Rome in the matter." Faced with Bernard's European-wide influence, even some bishops grew alarmed.

Misinformed by slanted reports or by intriguing churchmen, some cardinals of the Sacred Curia joined Bernard's enemies in denouncing him. "The Abbot's power has increased during the past years to an alarming degree," these disgruntled men told the pope, who ordered the chancellor of the Roman Church, Cardinal Haimeric, to remonstrate.

"You are meddling too much with things that a true monk has no business with," the cardinal wrote Bernard. "I advise you in the future to stay home, for it is unfitting that noisy, troublesome frogs should issue from their marshes to trouble the Holy See."

The reference to swamps and frogs brought a smile to Bernard's lips. He realized that he himself was the frog, accused of croaking too loudly to the world from the marshy fields of Clairvaux.

Only too willing to escape the charges so often laid on him by bishops, nobles, and scholars, Bernard sent a quick reply to the irate chancellor.

"I can see no one who can better spare me

such business in the future than Your Eminence, for you have the power and the willingness to do it. Henceforward, I beg you, act in such a way that both you and I may be content—you by maintaining order, and I by caring for the salvation of my soul. Let the troublesome frogs be forbidden to come out of their holes, ever to leave their marshes! Let them be heard no more in the councils and assemblies. Let neither need nor authority constrain them again to meddle in worldly affairs! That, perhaps, will bring to an end the accusations of pride and ambition brought against me. If by your authority, therefore, I can obtain the grace to remain always in my cloister, I shall live in peace and leave everybody else in peace too!"

Bernard's remarks touched the cardinal's heart and aroused his sense of justice. "The great Abbot of Clairvaux desires nothing but the hidden life of the true Cistercian," he announced to his confreres. "But Bernard's desires have been frustrated by events, as all of us well know. Hear, then, the real facts regarding the holy Abbot." The cardinal thereupon informed his colleagues how false accusers had misled them. As the truth filtered through all ranks of ecclesiastical society, all animosity against Abbot Bernard disappeared and his reputation shone more brightly than ever.

Surrounded by his monks at Clairvaux, Bernard patiently endured what God chose to send. "What a blessing our Abbot is to us," his monks admitted to one another. "The contemplative life, the instructions he gives us are his only concern. Yet the people bother him continually with their letters, their requests, their problems."

"The schools and universities," said Bernard's admirers, "send him learned questions he must answer, theological books he must approve. From everywhere come demands for his sermons, his writings."

"And what did the holy Abbot tell a prominent cardinal who requested certain of his books?" someone asked.

"I heard the answer from a good source," came the reply. Bernard told the cardinal: 'I have never, I think written any work of piety worthy of the attention of Your Eminence. Some religious, it's true, have collected fragments of sermons I've preached, which I now send you. Thus you will be cured of desire to read them.' "

In the twelfth century the problem of Church and State was even more complicated than it is today. Emperors and kings assaulted the rights of the papacy time and again. The struggle of the Church to free herself from the yoke of the empire reached its crisis during Bernard's lifetime.

"Investiture—the power of secular rulers to nominate bishops—can no longer be tolerated," said the Church leaders. "When princes give the bishop's ring and crozier, nothing but abuses can result, for unworthy men receive them and vacant sees are even sold to the highest bidder."

"Look how often the Church has protested against this evil. As far back as the General Councils of Nice and Constantinople three or four centuries ago, the practice of investiture has been forbidden, but to no effect. Now the episcopacy falls steadily into disrepute, and religion itself is being crippled."

"Too many bishops are feudal lords with

oaths of allegiance binding them to secular princes," said another spokesman.

"Yet bishops must have temporal power, too, lest confusion result and society fall into disorder. After all, they have cities, castles, and lands of their own to protect."

"It is for us," the pope told the cardinals, "to wrest the nomination of bishops from the overlords of the state, without yielding any civil authority the bishops hold. The struggle will be, as it's been for hundreds of years, long and bloody."

On the world's stage the forces of Church and State stood openly arrayed. When Henry V, the Emperor of Germany, died, there arose two claimants for the empty throne—Frederick Hohenstauffen and Lotharius of Saxony, and though the latter was finally elected, Frederick's brother Conrad prepared at once to dispute Lotharius' crown.

As if these disturbances were not enough, the death of Pope Honorius in the year 1130 gave rise to new disorders. The ambitious, wordly Cardinal Peter di Leone intrigued to capture the papal throne for himself, but the conclave chose Gregory, who took the name of Innocent II. Because several cardinals had not voted, Peter di Leone's party held an election of its own, naming their leader Pope Anacletus II. Thus a schism developed, with Christendom divided, allegiance of some leaders going to Innocent, of others to Anacletus. Innocent, the true pope, was forced to leave Rome, since all the city's strongholds were in the antipope's hands. Seeking support of the French king, Innocent appealed to a council summoned at Etampes, about twenty-five miles from Paris. Letters from the king and the bishops sped to Clairvaux, summoning Bernard. His examination of the election convinced him that Innocent was the legitimate pope, and the whole council universally acclaimed his choice. By command of the pope, Bernard continued his journeys in order to meet the German emperor and the king of England and win these monarchs over to the rightful pope's cause. Successful in both these missions, Bernard then induced Lothair to give up his power of investiture, a course of action Lothair decided upon because he hoped to receive the imperial crown from the pope's hands as Charlemagne had done four hundred years before. At Liege, in 1131, with Abbot Bernard attending, the Holy Roman Emperor walked humbly alongside the white donkey on which Pope Innocent rode, the king holding the bridle in one hand and clearing a way through the crowd with his sceptre in the other.

"If I grant the pope an army to lead him back to Rome, then I can claim the rights of investiture again," mused the emperor as he thrust his sceptre right and left among the throng.

"Though I am in a German city and surrounded by German men-at-arms," resolved the pope, "I will not compromise rights that belong to the Church alone."

With two such lords at odds, nothing but trouble would result, but Abbot Bernard managed to allay the storm. "What the crown demands is unjust, my lord," he told Lothair at a subsequent meeting. "Heed what you have formerly promised in this matter, and remember that if the Church at times needs the empire, the empire at all times needs the Church."

Much as he regretted it, Lothair finally gave up his claims, registering his dissatisfaction by breaking off plans for an Italian military campaign that would restore the pope safely in Rome. Innocent with his entourage now entered France and made a stop at the famous Abbey of Clairvaux, where the poor monks met the pontiff, not clad in purple and silk or carrying beautifully illuminated chant books, but clothed simply in their rough habits, with a plain, homely wooden cross at the head of the procession. No silver trumpets sounded, no cries of joy split the silence.

"These Cistercians break their profound silence only with psalms and hymns," the fine lords and ladies in the pope's train marveled, "nor do they look right or left. See, the pope himself weeps at the sight!"

In the refectory the guests were served coarse bread, herbs, and other simple dishes. For the pontiff, a dish of fish was readied, but only for him.

"Here there is not a banquet table," said His Holiness, "but a banquet of virtues."

In October, 1131, Bernard was summoned to a council of bishops at Rheims, where the pope himself presided. Louis-le-Gros, the French king, arrived with his queen, his sons, and grandees of the kingdom. As the king told Innocent of his eldest son's death, the pontiff admonished the ruler to submit to the will of God. "He has taken away your heir, an innocent lad, to make him reign henceforth in heaven; but he has left you other sons to reign here below in your place." The coronation of Louis-le-Jeune, who became Louis VII, followed in due course, with the pope annointing him with holy oil used in the consecration of French kings since the time of Clovis.

All the while the Council of Rheims sat, the Abbot Bernard kept busy with its affairs, and owing to his wise, tireless labors much work of reform was accomplished.

Just as the Council disbanded, Emperor Lothair promised two thousand soldiers to support the pope's return to Rome, news that sent the pontiff and Bernard to Italy to await their arrival. In city after city the holy Abbot preached peace, reconciled warring factions, and achieved more victories than a conquering army. Once Lothair had been crowned and the pope had achieved relative security in his domains, Innocent sent Bernard to Germany to reconcile Conrad with the Emperor. To humble the Hohenstauffen pride, Lothair demanded that Frederick and Conrad come in the garb of penitents to prostrate themselves before his throne in the presence of all the princes of the empire. The two proud men recoiling from such servility, Bernard stepped forth to urge their submission.

In the year 1135 the Abbot of Clairvaux, together with the Bishop of Chartres, traveled at the pope's behest to Aquitaine to confront the great Duke William.

"There is a man, powerful, haughty, who revels in schism and wantoness," said the bishop to his companion as they rode along. "He's strong as an ox, an able man of affairs, brilliant and formidable. But he lives for war, seeks every pleasure, and leads a life of sin. Worst of all, he stands in the lead of those supporting the anti-pope."

"His expelling the rightful bishops of two sees cannot be condoned," Bernard murmured, pondering what to do.

Stopping at a nearby monastery, Bernard sent a message to Duke William asking for a meeting. Agreeing, the prince of the realm talked with the holy Abbot for seven whole days, the wisdom and grace of Bernard's words melting the duke's hardened heart. Hardly had he returned to his castle, however, then courage and resolution failed him.

"I will close the wound Bernard has opened in my heart," cried the duke, "with even greater excesses than before!"

Four years passed before the burly lord of Aquitaine submitted, the schism growing meanwhile ever more violent. Once more the Abbot of Clairvaux appeared to reason with the sinful man, using threats and prayers to persuade the ruler to end his depradations.

"I will obey the lawful pope," the duke finally compromised, "but I will not consent to restoring the banished bishops to their sees."

Dissatisfied with the partial victory, Bernard

interrupted Mass one day when he reached the Kiss of Peace at the Agnus Dei. Laying the Sacred Host on the paten and with his face alight, Bernard walked down the nave of the church to confront the duke and his knights who, being excommunicated for their crimes, stood outside the church portals.

No longer pleading, but with a voice of authority, Bernard spoke in ringing tones: "We have long entreated you, yet you have despised us. Now behold! the Virgin's Son, Whom you persecute, comes to you—the Judge at Whose Name every knee bends in heaven, on earth, and in hell! Into His hands your soul, great duke, will fall! Will you despise the Lord Himself? Will you treat the Master as you have dealt with His servants?"

Astonished, the duke could say nothing, but the bystanders gasped in terror, quailing at the unprecedented sight. As the duke fell fainting, Bernard raised him up, led him to one of the banished bishops standing in the crowd. "Go, go immediately," the Abbot told the duke, "and be reconciled to those you have wrongfully driven out. Call back to unity all those who have fallen away."

Meekly the duke complied, leading the bishop to the cathedral throne and renouncing the schism once and for all. From a sinner steeped in crimes of all sorts, Duke William now became the instrument of the Divine Will, his change of heart clearly revealed to the whole of Aquitaine. Renouncing position and honors, he buried himself in solitude, where he disappeared from the world's eyes like an underground river. His daughter Eleanor, a woman notorious in years to come, received the duke's lands as dowry, a most fateful inheritance for subsequent decades. The great Duke William, however, spent his remaining years as a hermit and pilgrim, his home the wilderness, his happiness the things of God.

Continuing in various papal missions given him, Bernard traveled about France and Italy, always pursued by streams of people begging his help. He restored health to the sick, cured the crippled and maimed, drove out devils, and gave sight to the blind—becoming the instrument of hundreds of miracles wrought through the grace of God. Though he suffered pain and sickness almost uninterruptedly, he bore such things without complaint. His one desire was for solitude, the hidden life, the life of prayer, yet God made use of his exhausted body, his keen mind, and his mystic's soul to rule the destiny of Church and empire alike.

One day the people of Milan came in procession to his door, determined to force Bernard to accept the archiepiscopal throne of the diocese, then vacant. Knowing resistance to the excited crowd was dangerous, Bernard called out from a window.

"Tomorrow I'll mount my horse and let God decide the matter. If the horse takes me outside the walls, I shall consider myself free of the matter. But if the horse remains inside the walls, I will be your archbishop."

Next morning, Bernard did as planned, gave the horse his head, which, unreined and without a word of command, raced through the streets and out of the city.

On his return to Clairvaux, Bernard suffered

the loss of his brothers Guy and Gerard, both of whom died within a few months. At Gerard's funeral, the Abbot interrupted his discourse on the Canticles to exclaim: He was my brother by ties of blood, but more by bonds of religion. Pity my lot, you who know all this. I was weak in body and he supported me, timid and he encouraged me, slow and he helped me act."

In her last sickness Humbeline had the joy of a visit from her brother Bernard. He found her loved and respected among her nuns for the virtuous years she had spent in the convent. She died in August, 1141.

Four years later, the pretensions of antipopes finally settled, a monk from the Roman monastery of the Cistercians became Pope Eugenius III. For him Abbot Bernard wrote the book, *Of Considerations,* dealing with the duties of the Supreme Pontiff and a book that various popes through the centuries have used for meditation and enlightenment.

7

Two distinct schools of thought rose to the fore in the twelfth century: one, that faith is the source of real science and learning, and the other, that reason or human arguments alone provided the real fountainhead of knowledge.

The latter, Bernard believed, was a false philosophy. "It is the art of seeking the truth without ever finding it," he said.

"What we are confronted with," other scholars agreed, "is rationalism warring against the-

ology.   In former times human reason was sub-
ordinate to faith, but now men are trying to
make the human mind supreme in all things.
Why, the schools nowadays are making truth the
sport of reason, the plaything of logic.   Not even
the truths of faith escape their doubts and ques-
tionings."

Leader of the rationalist school was the great
scholar Abelard, next to Bernard the most learned man of the age. Informed of Abelard's errors,
Bernard wrote the man, but received an insulting
reply.

"Is it not enough that so many heresies
plague the Church at this time," said the bishops,
"with strange sects springing up on all sides who
have only one thing in common—hatred of the
Church!   Where is the man who can resist all
these dangerous trends?"

The Church leaders found the man in Abbot
Bernard, who bravely, almost with fury, took up
the fight.

"You will have giants of pride to contend
with," Bernard was told, "not only Abelard, but
outright heretics who attack religious instruc-

tion, oppose the Holy See, forbid marriage, deny the Sacraments, reject the Old Testament and the Church Fathers, and who even urge that the hierarchy be abolished."

"The heresies add up to one thing," said one bishop, "the open preaching of the downfall of Catholicism. Only the might of Bernard can stem the torrent."

The history of Abelard, and the refutation of his doctrine by Abbot Bernard form one of the most striking episodes of twelfth-century history. The love of Heloise and Abelard has been the source of romantic stories ever since, nor has the spectacle of reason and passion going astray together failed to titillate the world's fancy.

Abelard's attempt to arrive at truth merely by human reason, without faith, was the foundation of his error, as it is the error of all materialists.

"Divine faith is above and independent of the judgments of reason," Bernard and all orthodox theologians agreed. "But why do his notions attract so many scholars?"

"The answer lies in human nature, that

proud spirit of independence to which men are tempted," Bernard pointed out. "Abelard trusts in human power; we must trust in the power of God. The school of Abelard try to understand truth before they believe; we must believe before we can hope to understand."

"But are not my errors merely of words," Abelard asked his opponents, "since I respect the Church and believe what she teaches?"

"The danger of your teaching," he was told, "is subjecting dogmatic truths of faith to irresponsible questioning and discussion."

Though Abelard stood proudly before the world, his doctrines ever more popular, his career struck against two rock-like obstacles: against one he fell and was broken; the other crushed him by its weight. Heloise robbed him of the title of philosopher; Bernard destroyed his title of theologian.

Though Bernard sought him out, urging that Abelard abandon his false notions, the scholar refused to reform. Thoroughly aroused, Bernard warned bishops, cardinals, and pope of the dangerous situation. "Abelard accounts himself ready to give a reason for everything," the Abbot wrote. "He pretends to explain mysteries of faith that are above reason, saying they depend on human intellect alone for their truth or falsity."

"I protest these accusations," Abelard informed his powerful friends, "and demand to be heard in full council."

In 1140, on the octave of Pentecost, a great assembly of bishops and theologians gathered in Sens for a solemn debate between Bernard and Abelard, the two most celebrated persons of the time.

"Everyone looks on this conference as a kind of public spectacle," Bernard remarked.

"And is it not so?" asked his friends. "Will we not see a passage at arms, a duel, between men noted for eloquence; between two leaders who hold contrary ideas—one representing Divine authority and the other, the pre-eminence of human reason?"

The two champions appeared before the assembly, the list of accusations against Abelard were proclaimed, and, as the fathers of the council sat back to hear Abelard clear himself and defend his propositions, a mournful silence fell over the assembly.

The eyes of the crowd peering at him from every side, Abelard stammered, tried to speak, but words failed him.

"This is too much," he gasped, pointing to Bernard, standing in stern silence nearby.

After a few moments, Bernard stepped to the lectern to explain in detail the most glaring of the errors contained in Abelard's teaching. That done, he said, "I leave to Abelard the choice of retracting or defending his false ideas," but Abelard, still speechless, left the council, determined to appeal to the pope.

With unanimous voice the council condemned the scholar's mistaken notions, its judgment receiving papal approval in due course. Ordered to cease propagating heresy, Abelard submitted, published his retraction, and retired to a monastery.

"Abelard had nothing of the monk but the name and habit," Bernard said of him, "and he knows everything in heaven and on earth except himself!"

Bolder than their leader, certain disciples of Abelard continued spreading the false teaching, the spirit of their novel doctrines feeding the spirit of independence and rejection of divine revelation that still cause the world much disorder. A certain monk, Arnold of Brescia, spread the heresy with armed troops, first in France, then in Italy; but Bernard fought him at every turn. "Arnold of Brescia," he said, is a man who apparently neither eats nor drinks because like the devil he hungers only for the blood of souls. His conversation is sweet, but his doctrine is poison. He has the head of a dove but acts like a snake."

En route to confront the heresiarch on one occasion, Bernard stopped to bless some loaves brought him by the villagers. Making the sign of the Cross over them, he said, "By this shall you know the truth of our doctrine and the falsehood of that taught by the heretics: if the sick will eat these loaves, they will recover their health."

"You mean that if the sick eat and have faith,

they will be cured, don't you," asked Bernard's companion.

"Not so," the Abbot replied. "Be assured that they who eat will be cured. Thus will they know our authority comes from God and we preach His truth."

Alarming news now arrived in France from the East. Under Godfrey de Bouillon, knights of the First Crusade, some fifty years before, had captured the Holy Places in Palestine and set up a feudal kingdom there. The Franks built castles and fortresses, none strongly garrisoned but all surrounded by hostile Mohammedans. Disunited among themselves, the French nobles had little support from the Byzantine Emperor, the nearest Christian power; and they faced at all times the threat of inundation by the Moslem power. Finally, in 1144, the hordes of Islam, led by Ibn al Athir, stormed and captured the Christian outpost of Edessa, and won a victory of great political and religious importance for Islam.

Appeals to Byzantium brought no help, with the result that the Franks appealed to Rome, a step that aroused young King Louis VII to dreams of glory.

"Why not propose another Crusade?" he asked the pope.

Not enthusiastic, the cardinals pondered the matter at length. "The fall of Edessa puts Jerusalem and Antioch both under threat of defeat," they agreed. "Jerusalem is a name that inspired the world; it might do so still. And was not the First Crusade fought not so much for possession of the Holy Places as for who will govern the souls of men—Christ or Mohammed? Does not Europe itself tremble without letup before the victories of Islam? Perhaps the only way to fight the danger is to unite Christendom once again in a common effort."

The discussion in high places continued, yet the French king did not act. Finally, the Pope, Eugenius III, determined to appeal to the Christian nobles to defend the conquests of their fathers.

"But a spark for such a venture is lacking," the pontiff mused. "The knights know only too well from tales of the First Crusade what obstacles and sufferings a holy war would bring. Let us call on Abbot Bernard to give impetus, to preach a new crusade and at the same time to grant the same indulgences given the crusaders of old."

A great parliament was convoked at Vezelay in Burgundy at which Bernard was to sound the first trumpet-call for the Second Crusade. To it came Louis-le-June, his queen Eleanor of Aquitaine, the lords and princes of the realm, all of them anxious to receive the crusaders' cross from Bernard's hands.

A man of fifty-four years at this time, Bernard took on the great labor of preaching the crusade though he tottered with weakness and his body was worn out with self-denial and suffering.

"How can he hope to convince Frenchmen to join in the venture," certain nobles wondered. "Everyone's busy these days building cathedrals—there's one in almost every French town. I'll wager his job will be twice as hard as Peter the Hermit's, he who preached the First Crusade to our fathers."

Fired with zeal for the mission given him by the pope, Bernard had prepared the way by writing fiery letters to people of influence and position.

Now, on the brow of a hill chosen for the parliament, the crowd gathered, for no church was big enough, no town square spacious enough to hold the multitude. With young Louis VII, the King of France, the Abbot ascended the platform, holding aloft a crusader's cross of red cloth. Even before he began reading the pope's proclamation, the crowd shouted again and again, "The Cross! The Cross!"

Halfway through his declaration of the summons to holy war, Bernard had to stop, the crowd interrupting with cries of "It is the will of God! It is the will of God!"

Now the king cast himself at Bernard's feet, vowing in the presence of all to march to assist the Holy Land. As the king called his warriors around him, the lords, barons, bishops, the queen herself, stepped forward to receive the Cross. Lacking enough of these, Bernard tore his own cloak to make temporary crosses of the fragments.

In the days following, enthusiasm for the new crusade continued to mount. "The movement has begun in earnest," the lords agreed.

"It is the spirit of God that triumphs," the abbot told them. "Let old grievances now be laid aside, let peace treaties be made between warring barons, and let all local wars come to speedy end."

Some of his monks puzzled over the warlike attitude of their gentle Abbot. Fortunately, explanations were soon made by wise monks who understood. "Our abbot seeks order in Christendom," they said, "the bringing of divine authority to bear in men's affairs. Bernard calls on the Christian nations to defend the order established by God and he preaches the holy war with this one principle in mind. The forming of alliances among princes and all other matters he leaves to the princes."

"In French baronies, duchies, and other provinces," said one of the monks, "the lords set aside their old grievances and make treaties of peace, at least until they return from the crusade.

The king has set the departure date for next spring."

Bernard's thoughts during these exciting days centered oftentimes on the Holy City, so much loved by Christians. "Hail to thee," he wrote of it, "Queen of nations, capital of empires, see of patriarchs, mother of prophets and apostles, first cradle of our faith, the glory and honor of Christianity." As in the First Crusade, the eyes of all Europe looked once more to Jerusalem, the city no one could forget.

When the assembly at Vezelay dispersed, the Abbot Bernard journeyed through Burgundy and neighboring provinces to enroll other soldiers under the standard of the cross. "He's like Moses, sent to lead the Chosen People to the Promised Land," said the womenfolk as they watched their husbands' wild response to Bernard's fiery sermons.

"Let Abbot Bernard march at the head of all French knights," declared the expedition leaders of Chartres; "with him in command, we cannot fail."

"Such a role ill befits a simple monk," Bernard responded, turning aside at once to write the pope, who quickly accepted the abbot's refusal.

The German provinces, meanwhile, shared in the general enthusiasm for a new crusade. Hating the Saracens, the infidel unbelievers who rejected Christ, certain fanatics in German lands began persecuting the Jews, whom they believed no better than Mohammedans. From France, Bernard wrote stinging rebukes to the persecutors, his letters not only extolling the Jews but setting forth the merits of the crusade he had been commissioned to preach.

Finally, the Abbot entered the fray in person, convinced the only hope for the crusade lay in France and Germany. Day after day he labored for the cause. "This servant of God," said Bernard's companion Godfrey, "works miracles more easily than I can write about them. His breath, his blessing, the touch of his hand, his very presence—these bring sight to the blind, cure the deaf and dumb, restore paralytics, and drive out evil spirits. Greatest of all, Bernard melts the hardened hearts of sinners, even the greatest of whom do their public penance without quailing."

The Emperor Conrad III, who had succeeded Lothair on the German throne, met the abbot at Metz. "But, my good Father, nothing is further from my mind than going on crusade," he told Bernard mildly. "I have all sorts of disturbances here at home to contend with and dare not leave these lands."

Urged by Conrad to remain a while longer despite this disappointing news, Bernard confronted a huge crowd one day in a church at Metz, the whole throng pressing ahead to see the face of the man they believed a saint. Seeing Bernard in danger of being smothered, the emperor threw off his mantle, lifted the poor worn abbot in his powerful arms, and bore him to safety. The moment was opportune for a mild reproach. "Why is it the people demand the cross, yet the princes waver?" Bernard asked his rescuer.

On Christmas Day the city of Squires lay decked with banners and garlands, ready to welcome Bernard, the pope's envoy, who was to attend the Diet called by Emperor Conrad. In procession the bishop, the clergy, and the towns-people came to the gates. To pealing bells and rousing hymns the marchers led Bernard to the cathedral where the emperor, with the leading princes of the realm, waited to receive him. The choir sang the beautiful hymn, *"Salve Regina,"* as the procession advanced from the portal to the choir. Just as the last echoes of the *"Salve"* died away, the holy abbot rapturously cried out: *"O clemens! O pia! O dulcis Virgo Maria!"* words which have been included in Our Lady's anthem ever since: "O merciful, O loving, O sweet Virgin Mary!"

In the assembly, or Diet, later in the day, Bernard found Emperor Conrad still hesitant about joining the holy war. A short time after-ward, while he celebrated Mass in the presence of the court, the abbot mounted the pulpit to deliver an impassioned address on the woes of the Holy Land.

"Think of the crusade as a simple soldier, not as a sovereign," he told the vacillating ruler. "Consider the graces and gifts God has granted you, and fear lest you prove ungrateful. What, my lord, will you answer in the day of judgment if you refuse when God calls?"

Struck suddenly to the heart by Bernard's piercing words, Emperor Conrad stepped forward to demand the crusader's cross. "I admit that God gives me many graces," he declared, weeping, "and with His help, I will try to be worthy of them. Wherever God calls, there I shall go."

At once cries of acclamation filled the cathedral. From Bernard's hand Conrad received the proud banner standing in the sanctuary, and at the same moment all the German princes knelt at Bernard's feet to beg for the red cross, among them Frederick Barbarossa, the heir to Conrad's throne. Ensuing meetings of the Diet turned now on the fate of Jerusalem, not on disorders in Germany. "That alone is a miracle of miracles," admitted the barons. "And what a marvel it is that thieves and bandits even vow they'll shed their blood for Christ in the venture."

Like a sculptor carving a statue, certain men shape their age. The impulse for the Second

Crusade came from Bernard, spread first in France, then throughout Europe. East and West prepared to battle as Asia trembled, and out of the bloody shock rose the modern world.

"Now that Bernard's raised two formidable armies," a cardinal of the Roman Rota remarked one day, "might he not deserve a little rest?"

"Abbot Bernard is a man whose eagle glance takes in vast horizons," another said. "He realized only too well that Conrad's absence from Germany would make easy pickings of the crown among greedy German lords. Only the other day, I received news that the Duke of Bavaria has promised to take the cross, along with the prelates and barons. Otho of Frisingen, Duke Ladislaus of Bohemia, the Marquis of Styria, and many other princes have vowed to do the same, to fight the infidels. Friend and foe alike encamps together in the holy cause."

"Now that dozens of small wars in Europe have ended," said one old cardinal, "a profound silence reigns throughout the West. Indeed, people consider it a crime to bear arms for any reason except the coming crusade."

On the fourth of January, 1147, the Abbot Bernard gave his farewell speech to the German emperor, princes, and crusader battalions, all of whom crowded close to pay him their last homage. Townsmen and country folk lined the streets to watch the brilliant army begin its march. Riding alongside Emperor Conrad, Bernard leaned over to touch a crippled child who called to him, and as the boy rose instantaneously healed, the monarch gasped with surprise.

"It is on your account that God has wrought this cure," Bernard told him. "Thus you may know that God is with you and your undertaking pleases Him."

In the city of Cologne, where the marchers arrived after a journey down the Rhine, the crowds before Bernard's lodging grew so huge that the sick had to be presented to him on ladders. "We dare not open the doors because of the crush," the stout bearers explained. "In fact, good Father, your brother Gerard has been waiting in the street since nine o'clock this morning without being able to enter the house, and it's dusk now."

A string of wonders marked Bernard's progress through the countryside and towns. "We can hardly go a step without something occurring," Gerard wrote the monks back at Clairvaux. "The crowd follows us everywhere, and the fields are as full of people as the towns."

Godfrey, another companion of the abbot's agreed. "I ascertained the fact that on one particular day our holy father had healed on the road one blind girl, three deaf persons, one cripple, and after that, five blind men."

The German troops having proceeded eastwards, Bernard arrived at Chalons-sur-Marne in France on February 2, where the assembly of French princes, Louis the king, and the ambassadors from Germany escorted him into the city with honors due a papal envoy. After a short stay at Clairvaux, the abbot rejoined the noble assembly, now convoked at Etampes. The presence of Bernard rekindled the waning spirits of the knights, and by his help the French were granted permission to freely pass across Germany and Hungary on the way east. A letter from the Byzantine Emperor Manuel Comnenus heartened the leaders with its promise of friend-ship, for they knew how the Greeks had ham-pered marchers in the First Crusade.

"The only and quickest route is by sea," said the warriors from Sicily. The sea route will bring you to Syrian ports in a few weeks, but a land-march means many months before any troops could arrive."

Unfortunately, the counsel of the Sicilians, though prompted by greed for profit to be made by transporting the crusaders, did not prevail. The French decided to march through the Dan-ube valley and reach Constantinople on foot.

"But what of my kingdom?" inquired Louis-le-Jeune, busy with his council in finding some-one to administer French affairs during his absence.

After full deliberation of this problem with the king's men, Bernard stepped forward in the council chamber and gestured toward Abbot Suger, who had served so long as Louis' minister, and the Count of Never. "Behold the two swords which we have chosen," said the abbot; "They are sufficient."

Having made plans to enter a monastery months before, the Count resisted the appointment, despite the king's protests.

"Nor do I want the dignity of regent—really a burden rather than an honor," said Abbot Suger.

The king's wishes, along with those of the pope, finally prevailed; the Abbot Suger became regent of all France, and the crusaders could now plan their departure.

"The whole country seems to be on the move," remarked Suger's attendants as they accompanied him to Paris. "We've hardly seen anyone but men wearing the red cross, traveling to join their leaders. Only pilgrims and troubadours are left on the roads."

"I've learned that knights who refuse to join the crusade are given a spindle and distaff," another courtier remarked, "as token of ridicule. And why not! They are no better than weak women!"

Pope Eugenius now published startling news. "Let us go to France to see the great things Bernard has done," he declared, for the holy war was never far from his mind.

In a few weeks the papal cortege arrived at Dijon where the King of France waited with his brilliant court. At sight of the pontiff, the king dismounted, threw himself at the pope's feet.

"I accept this homage in the name of Jesus Christ, Whose place I hold," Eugenius declared solemnly, continuing with praiseworthy remarks for the royal family.

"The greatest problem of the crusade is to raise money to meet the enormous expenses," the king informed His Holiness. "While pious gifts are considerable, they are not enough to maintain an army. I've borrowed and taxed to the limit; but the noblemen have little money even though they are rich in land."

"Sell franchises granting certain freedoms to the communes and merchants," the king was advised—advice which, eventually followed, planted thriving seeds of liberty in the hearts of even the lowliest of the king's subjects.

8

Plans for the crusade called for the French
warriors to meet in the town of Metz, the Germans in Ratisbonne. With great pomp Conrad
with his nobles, including the most elite of the
Teutonic knights, marched from the city clad in
shining armor of gold or steel, the 70,000
lances glittering in the sun, the earth trem-
bling under the hoofs of their horses. Outside
the walls the troops wound over the open plain,
the ensigns and colors floating overhead, the

casques, cuirasses, and bucklers of silver shining in the sun. Besides the nobles and their squires, there were light horse bands, foot soldiers, and pilgrims of both sexes. The German army was to march across Hungary and Bulgaria, making its camp near Constantinople to await the arrival of the French.

As departure time approached for the Franks, the Most Christian King Louis VII meekly proceeded to put his spiritual house in order. With only two servants, he visited all the nearby religious houses to give alms. To the poor he also opened his purse, and the lepers he served with his own hands. At the church of St. Denis, where the entire court had assembled, the king received the pilgrim's staff and scrip from the pope.

Next morning the 100,000 crusaders of France, along with foot soldiers and pilgrims, began the march eastward, a long two months after the German troops had set out.

From this moment the crusade that Bernard had preached so brilliantly began to fall apart. Conrad's army not only lacked discipline, but the countries it crossed harassed the marchers by withholding supplies, giving false directions, and in other inimical ways. In November, 1147, Mohammedan troops surrounded the Germans, cutting them to pieces, with whole divisions tricked into positions where they were unable to do battle. Though the Bishop of Langres had advised the capture of Constantinople, the emperor refused to take action, giving Manuel Comnenus opportunity to intrigue with the Turks and reveal the Latins' plans. With his army nearly destroyed around him, Emperor Conrad had no other course than to return, a beaten man, to his own kingdom.

The course of the war was equally dark for the French. By the year 1148 Louis had advanced far into Greece, but the treachery of certain of his commanders resulted in his rearguard being cut to shreds. Only with difficulty did the king himself escape the slaughter. With a small band of troops he pushed forward to a seaport town, where he embarked for Antioch, but he left behind the major part of his forces who mouldered away for want of provisions and because of Greek treachery. Troubled by the scandalous behavior of his queen, Eleanor of Aquitaine, Louis nonetheless proceeded with the siege of Damascus, an enterprise that failed because certain Christian lords became jealous during the venture. Finally, the French king like his German counterpart, gave up the crusade and returned to his kingdom. He had marched away with a hundred thousand men, but he returned with only a few hundred knights. Hardly a family in the kingdom but had suffered loss.

"The finger of God is visible in this disaster," said the Abbot of Clairvaux. "The crusade failed not so much because the Greeks were treacherous, but because the crusaders themselves failed to live up to their holy quest. Greed, murder, scandal seems to have been their business, not holy war."

The failure of the crusade covered Bernard's great fame with a black cloud. Looked on so long as the oracle of the Church, the arbiter of divine and human things, he now became in the world's eyes an imposter and false prophet.

"Bernard stirred up the holy war," said the

angry people, "he preached it, backed it with wonders and miracles. But now the Christian armies are destroyed and nothing but bad news comes from the East. Bernard has ruined France and Germany both. He's betrayed the Church itself."

The public outcry left the holy abbot unmoved, his interior peace of soul undisturbed. "I have never acted except at the command of God and the Holy See," he explained to his friends, who came to commiserate with him. "Now I leave all things in the hands of God— my person, my reputation, my work."

"Surely your cup is bitter," said his companions. "It seems that the good Lord wishes you to drink it to the dregs!"

Time gradually calmed the storm brought on by the disastrous Second Crusade, the truth regarding it spread to all quarters of Europe.

"Actually, it is the monasteries and the crusades," the learned historians finally managed to explain, "that brought society out of barbarism and disorder that marked the tenth and eleventh centuries so terribly. Before the holy wars took place, and even as they were fought, Islam was spreading everywhere, even into Christian lands like Spain, Sicily, and north Africa. Christians could only dare attack successfully in its very heart—in Asia, to prevent Islam conquering the world. Remember, too, that in the crusades soldiers of the Faith gave their lives in expiation of their sins. Thus by dying for the cause of Christ these men triumphed over themselves."

The worst humiliation that Bernard suffered in these years came not from the debacle of the crusade but from a monk of Clairvaux, Nicholas, who worked as the abbot's secretary and whom he trusted with important business of the monastery.

"But what do I discover, now that I've returned!" Bernard exclaimed to his council. "The monk Nicholas has carved a false seal, using this stamp on letters he's written over my name to recommend certain unworthy men to the Holy See for advancement."

"Nicholas feared confronting you, good Abbot," said the council spokesman. "He's since fled to England, but reports have disclosed the fact that his attacks on your reputation, his calumnies, continue worse than ever."

"False accusations don't bother me, but we must take action at once to correct the harm he's done."

Bernard explained matters more fully in a letter to the pope. "Besides books, gold, and silver which Nicholas carried away, he stole three seals—his own, the prior's, and mine. Using my seal, he's addressed letters to the Court of Rome that were full of lies. I dare not defile my lips and your ears by listing all the crimes Nicholas has committed."

To avoid future difficulties of this sort, Abbot Bernard changed his official seal, having engraved on it his name and personal mark.

Aware how even men of high rank scorned the meek, humble Abbot of Clairvaux during these angry days following the crusade, a cleric appeared to demand admittance to the monastery, a request Bernard refused because of the man's imperious manner.

"What good is it then," the cleric blustered, "to recommend perfection in your books when you deny it to people seeking for it? Why, if I had a book of yours at hand right now, I'd tear it to pieces!"

"I don't think you've read in any books of mine," Bernard said firmly, "that you can't become perfect at home. Change of manners, of life, is what I recommended, not change of place."

The cleric, wild with rage, struck the abbot on the cheek so hard that it reddened and swelled. Monks who had witnessed this sacrilege sprang forward, furious, to check the man.

"Let him go," Bernard ordered at once. "I beg you, friends, in the name of Jesus, do not harm the fellow, but let him go in peace."

Gradually, the "season of disgrace," as Bernard called it, began to grow brighter, and people came to understand that the crusade failed because of their own shortcomings and not because Bernard lacked wisdom and forethought in promoting the venture. The principle behind the holy wars remained pure and sacred, notwithstanding disasters that obscured their glory.

By mid-century the great reform and the renewal of society inaugurated by leaders of Church and State were firmly established, but some of Christendom's most eminent personages now began disappearing from the scene. First to die was the Abbot Suger, Bernard's old friend, who grieved deeply over the fate of the crusade. Suger's plans to raise troops in his own name and to march himself at their head to Jerusalem never materialized because a serious illness brought the abbot to bed, never to rise.

Summoning the most courageous and experienced knight he knew, Suger charged him to swear to serve in Jerusalem in the place the abbot himself longed to serve.

Bernard sent the dying Suger a comforting letter, telling his friend. "I beg you to believe," he wrote, "that having loved you so long, I shall never cease to love you. I do not lose you; I only send you before me to our Lord."

The incorruptible Suger, a model minister of state and true "father of his country," died in the year 1152, at the age of seventy. The eulogy Abbot Bernard pronounced on receiving word of his friend's death admirably summed up a lifetime: "If there be any precious vessel adorning the palace of the King of kings, it is without doubt the soul of the venerable Suger."

Other illustrious names soon were being carved on tombs, reminders to Bernard and to the world that even the noblest figures of history quickly come to dust.

Now Bernard himself approached the end of his career, and more than ever "his conversation was in heaven." Shortly after the New Year of 1153, his old maladies returned in full force, yet he continued to offer Mass daily.

"His words seem more rare and penetrating than ever before," his monks remarked to one another. "And do you notice how often, after Mass, a light seems to surround our holy father's head. Whenever you draw near him, love and fervor spring to heights you didn't know existed."

Of course, the community begged God to spare their abbot a while longer, but Bernard called his large family around him. "Why would you keep me here on earth. You've prayed that I grow stronger, and strength has returned. But your victory is against my desire. Show me even greater charity, I beg you, and let me depart to God."

To one of his dearest friends, Bernard addressed his last letter. "I have received with much gratitude the tokens of esteem you sent me. But nothing gives me pleasure anymore, for what joy can a man taste who suffers overwhelmingly? I have no moment of respite, even when I eat nothing at all. Like Job, I can say that sleep never comes, lest I stop feeling pain. My stomach can no longer endure food, yet pains when empty. My feet and legs are swollen with dropsy. But because I conceal nothing from you, let me say that my soul sinks not; my body is weak, but the spirit is ready. Pray to our Lord, who desires not the death of sinners, to help me as I leave this world and not to delay taking me, for it is time for me to die. Aid with your prayers a man devoid of all merit, that in this momentous hour the devil may not triumph over me. I have desired to write you with my own hand to show how much I love you, and that when you recognize my handwriting, you may also recognize my heart. But I should have been much better pleased to have spoken than to have written."

Six weeks before Bernard's death came the sorrowful news that Pope Eugenius, formerly one of his own dear Cistericians, died peacefully after a reign of eight and a half years. During his pontificate, the primacy of St. Peter resummed its vivifying influence in the world's affairs.

The news, quite unexpected, left Bernard bereft of his last consolation, for he loved the pope deeply and tenderly. Each passing day left the holy abbot farther away from things occurring around him.

Visiting the monastery to consult Bernard on some affair, the Bishop of Langres could not conceal his surprise at the little attention Bernard paid to his remarks.

"Do not trouble me any more," the abbot said gently. "I am no longer of this world."

"Truly, that is so," the bishop told the monks outside the abbot's cell. "Bernard seeks only to loosen the last threads that bind him to this earthly life. His entire soul, all his attention, are concentrated on God, his love and delight. Desire, yes, desire, has already brought your abbot to heaven."

Plainly, Bernard was on his death-bed, yet the Archbishop of Treves came to Clairvaux to beg his help.

"Horrible events are assailing the province of Metz," said the archbishop, kneeling by Bernard's bed. "Nobles are fighting the commoners, and already more than two thousand people have perished in the wars. The combatants refuse to listen to me, to let me mediate between them. I had but one resource — to call the Abbot of Clairvaux to the battlefield. Only you, good father, can pacify these angry souls."

Bernard longed to help, and God willed he do so. Miraculously strength returned, his energies revived, and he rose from bed to journey to Metz, where the two opposing forces were encamped on opposite sides of the river. Supported by some fellow monks, Bernard visited each camp, talked to the leaders, but had little hope of success.

"It's only your presence on the field," he was told, "that suspends the shock of arms."

"Do not fear," the abbot told his monks, "for

I promise you'll see order restored."

In the middle of the night a deputation of nobles appeared, promising to accept Bernard's mediation, and shortly after dawn representatives of both camps met on a little river island with the Abbot of Clairvaux. Warrior leaders of the various troops sat in their boats, ringing the shore.

Carefully Abbot Bernard listened to the grievances of both sides, then his wise words of counsel gave satisfaction to the warring parties. The fighters laid down their arms, and the kiss of peace was passed throughout the camps.

"We cannot fail to hear a man so loved by God," said the leaders. "We will heed his advice."

. Once more Bernard retired humbly to Clairvaux, lying once more in pain on the hard pallet to peacefully await his deliverance.

Seeing their abbot dying, the monks hoped against hope, for they loved their father blindly. Bernard promised not to abandon them, even after his death. "But I beg and entreat you," he urged his subjects, "in the name of our Lord

Jesus Christ, that as you have learned from us to live and to please God, you continue in the same way and grow more and more in holiness. For, remember always, the will of God is that you become saints."

The Superior General of the Cistercians, with other abbots and prelates, arrived at Clairvaux to pay their last visit. Bernard thanked them all, and in a weak voice, bade them farewell. He knew that they were all storming heaven with prayers for his recovery.

"Why do you detain a wretched sinner here below," he asked.

They did not answer his question. They had not the heart to do so, for they well knew his love for God and his desire to be with Him made him desire to leave this wretched world.

"Your prayers have prevailed upon me. But know this, my sons: the good God grants me but another six months to live."

The monks were now happy. Bernard's face brightened, and a bit of color showed in his hollow cheeks. But life meant work. And for some time thereafter, Bernard continued to carry on the strenuous work of his office, and helped all who came to him.

But his monks remembered his prophecy, and as the months passed, they noticed their abbot and friend slowing down gradually.

"Life will not be the same once Father Bernard is gone," one of them said.

"We must storm heaven again for his recovery," another added. "Who knows but that God will hear our prayer again."

Prayers, of course, were said, and each day the monks looked in vain for some slight change in the abbot's face or step, but they found none.

Then the day came when Bernard's old sickness returned, and he was forced to bed. This time, he knew, there would be no recovery.

His own monks lost their control as they stood by his bedside. "Father," they cried, "will you then leave us? Have you no pity on us, your children? What will become of all your work, of us whom you loved so well?"

"I know not to which I ought to yield," Bernard whispered, looking up with angelic kindness, "whether to the love of my children, which urges me to remain here, or to the love of my God, which draws me to Him."

These were Bernard's last words. To tolling bells and funeral chants intoned by the seven hundred monks at Clairvaux, 'the death of the great Abbot of Clairvaux was announced to the world. His final moment came about nine o'clock in the morning, on August 20, 1153.

Those who were present at his holy death knew Bernard so well that they felt his soul speed straight to heaven. They grieved for his loss because he had been a real father to them, but the thought that he was now with God and would be a powerful intercessor for them, made them feel great peace in their souls.

9

Abbot Bernard was sixty-three years old at his death; he had been a Cistercian monk for forty years and held the office of abbot for all but two years of his religious life. Behind him he left not only Clairvaux with its seven hundred monks, but one hundred and sixty other Cistercian monasteries, dotting the countries of Europe and Asia.

The monks buried their abbot before the altar of Our Lady at Clairvaux. Only twelve years later Pope Alexander III enrolled him among the saints.

One of St. Bernard's favorite bits of advice was that a man should learn exactly who he is, why he is here, and where he is going. He even had a word for those modern men who think science has all the answers.

"Many men know many things," he said. "They measure the heavens, count the stars, pretend to dive into mysteries of faith and into the secrets of nature. But their science is all folly and empty vanity because they do not know themselves. Consequently, such men have not learned the first elements of the science of the saints. Knowledge that leads only to pride drives the Holy Spirit with His gifts out of the soul. The most illiterate idiot is more capable of receiving the Holy Spirit and His wisdom than such men. The key to holiness, then, is to have a deep sense of a man's own nothingness, of his weakness, sinfulness, unworthiness. A man must improve the knowledge of himself by perfecting his knowledge of God — His greatness, goodness, mercy, glory, and other infinite perfections.

Just as a single ray of sunlight gives more light on earth than all the stars put together so one ray of heavenly light shows a man what he is better than his own study and reflection can possibly do. This knowledge comes through contemplation and prayer, the only means of learning about God. Thus we must pray with St. Augustine: "Lord, teach me to know Thee, and to know myself."

St. Bernard has been called "the last of the Fathers," which means he ranks with such men as St. Augustine and St. Ambrose among early teachers and writers of the Church.

Like other great saints, St. Bernard's story can hardly be told without telling the history of his own time. He above all exemplifies the power of an individual man over the course of events during a given period of time. There was Bernard — a solitary monk, poor, without rank or office, without worldly ambition or influence; yet he achieved sway and power not only over his own monastic foundations and their hundreds of monks, but over people of every character, rank, and talent; over priests, bishops, and popes;

over kings and princes, kingdoms and nations.
Why?

The reason must be sought within Bernard's own great heart, within the walls of his monastic cell. Bernard accomplished what he did because he loved God; he burned with love of Him. His intelligent mind was illumined by the light of Faith; his strong will was made inflexible by union with Christ.

Holy and mortified religious that he was, yet Bernard became one of the most powerful personages of the twelfth century. He appeared in the schools, at the altar, in the pulpits, in the councils of Church and State, in governmental affairs, among warring cities, in contests between popes and antipopes.

Where did he get the power to deal with such affairs?

Not from training for it in the schools of the world, to be sure. His power and influence stemmed from his immersion in God. The supernatural was his guide in all things: to learn and to follow what God willed.

St. Bernard, like so many other saints —

Anselm, Francis, Bonaventure, Peter Damien, Alphonsus, and others, stands as a witness to a great spiritual law: that love of the Virgin Mother of God is not a sentiment or poetry in religion, but a profound source of true piety. From St. Bernard men learn once again that love and veneration of the Blessed Virgin Mary is a law springing from the very substance of the Faith.

Of all writers who lived during the first thousand years of Christianity, none is more fervent, tender, adoring in his love for our Divine Lord than St. Bernard, and none is more conspicuous for his love of the Mother of God.

Let Bernard, then, speak the final word about the love of God.

"Why should we love God?"

"Because He is God."

"How much, with what measure, should we love God?"

"Love Him without measure."

CPSIA information can be obtained
at www.ICGtesting.com
Printed in the USA
BVHW042317150223
658635BV00010B/200